JAPANESE HOMESTYLE COOKING

Tokiko Suzuki

GRAPH-SHA / Japan Publications

FOR BEGINNERS OF JAPANESE CUISINE

Japanese cuisine is easy to prepare at home. One of its characteristics is to make much of the four distinct seasons, taking advantage of the various foods available at each time of the year. Foods in season are appetizing and are available at reasonable prices. The first step of Japanese cuisine is to get seasonal ingredients.

Do your best to serve palatable Japanese dishes to others, taking care to be clean in everything. Put your heart and soul into the arrangement of the food.

At first you will find it difficult to prepare Japanese dishes, but you can master it after repetition. It is worth trying with all your heart.

Tokiko Suzuki

CONTENTS

For Beginners of
  Japanese Cuisine.................... 3

Kitchen Equipment 6
Basic Cutting Techniques........ 10

SIMMERED DISHES

Braised Chicken...................... 14
Braised Beef and Potatoes........ 16
Assortment of Simmered Foods 18
Flatfish Cooked Quickly 20
Simmered Kinmedai................. 22
Simmered Mackerel in Miso 23
Simmered Pork with Daikon
  Radish 24
Simmered Turnips with Minced
  Chicken 26
Kamaboko and Mitsuba Cooked
  with Eggs........................... 27
Nabe-shigi of Eggplant 28
Burdock Kimpira..................... 29
Nibitashi of Komatsuna and
  Aburage 30
Nibitashi of Chinese Cabbage
  and Littleneck Clams 31
Nibitashi of Lettuce and Young
  Sardines 31
Simmered Kidney Beans 32
Hijiki Mixed with Vegetables..... 33
Dried Strips of Daikon Radish   34
■Tips for Simmered Dishes 36

BROILED AND PAN-FRIED DISHES

Salt-broiled Horse Mackerel 38
Salt-broiled Yellowtail 39
Spanish Mackerel with
  Yuan-jiru 40
Broiled cuttlefish with Egg Yolk
  41
Broiled Pomfret in Saikyo-way 42
●Variations of Broiled Foods ... 43
Beef Tataki............................. 44
Chicken Teriyaki 45
Thick Omelets......................... 46
●Omelets with Fillings 47
■Tips for Broiled and Pan-fried
  Dishes 48

DEEP-FRIED DISHES

Tempura 50
●Tentsuyu (tempura sauce)..... 50
●Variations of Batter.............. 52
Mixed Tempura of Kobashira
  and Mitsuba 54
●Variations of Mixed Tempura 55
Deep-fried Marinated Pork 55
Deep-fried Puffy Tofu 56
Deep-fried Pond Smelts in
  Nanban-zu 57
■Tips for Deep-fried Dishes..... 58

STEAMED DISHES

Steamed Egg Custard............... 60
●Custard in a Bowl 61
Steamed Tilefish and Turnip 62
Chiri-mushi of Bluefish............ 63
■Tips for Steamed Dishes 64

VINEGARED AND DRESSED DISHES

Chrysanthemum Turnip in
  Ama-zu 66
Ark Shells and Rape Blossoms
  with Nihai-zu 67
Cucumber and Wakame with
  Sanbai-zu 67
Cuttlefish and Cucumber with
  Kimi-zu 68
Udo and Broad Beans in Ume
  Dressing 69
Octopus and Butterbur with
  Karashi-zu 69
Round Clams and Scallions
  with Karashi Su-miso........... 70
Bamboo Shoot and Cuttlefish
  with Kinome-miso 71
Horse Mackerel and Negi with
  Su-miso 72
Tofu Dressing......................... 72
Spinach with Sesame Dressing 74
String Beans with Sesame
  Dressing 75
Rape Blossoms Dressed in Soy
  Sauce with Mustard.............. 75
Soy-steeped Spinach 76
Soy-steeped Mitsuba 77
Soy-steeped Asparagus and
  Shiitake 77

■Tips for Vinegared and
  Dressed Dishes 78

SASHIMI DISHES

Sashimi 80
Vinegared Mackerel................. 84
Chopped Horse Mackerel......... 85
■Tips for Sashimi Dishes 86

ONE POT DISHES

Assorted Casserole.................. 88
Sukiyaki 90
Oden...................................... 92
■Tips for One Pot Dishes........ 94

RICE AND NOODLES

Mixed Sushi............................ 96
Thick Sushi Rolls 98
Stuffed Tofu Puff Sushi 100
Red Bean Rice........................ 101
Rice with Vegetables.............. 102
Buckwheat Noodles with
  Tempura 104
Wheat Noodles with Bonito
  Flakes 104
Fine Noodles 104
●Broth and Dipping Sauce 105
■Tips for Rice and Noodles 106

SOUPS

Miso Soups
  Asparagus and Udo............. 110
  Okra and Tofu.................... 110
  Shimeji Mushrooms and
    Tofu 111
  Gurnard and Burdock......... 111
Clear Soups
  Vegetable Soup 112
  Sea Bass and Harusame
    Soup................................. 112
  Mushrooms and Curdled
    Egg Soup 113
  Scallops and Vegetable
    Soup................................. 113
■Tips for Soups 114

◆Seasonal Ingredients........... 116

All the recipes are for 2 servings, unless otherwise specified.

SPRING MENUS

Colorful Spring Dishes
Tosa-ni of Bamboo Shoot and
    Butterbur............................ 120
Rape Blossoms and Udo in
    Karashi-zu 120
Grilled Scabbard Fish 121
Clear Bamboo Shoot Soup...... 121

Enjoy the Savor of Spring
Cabbage and Radishes
    Squeezed with Salt 122
Simmered Zenmai 122
Beef, Broad Beans and Udo.... 123
Pan-fried Clams 123

Spring Dishes in Small Bowls
Pounded Bracken................... 124
Cabbage Simmered with
    Vinegar 124
Green Peas Thickened with
    Kuzu.................................. 124
Mitsuba and Chicken with
    Wasabi Vinegar 125
Taranome with Sesame
    Dressing 125
Kimpira of Udo Skin.............. 125

SUMMER MENUS

A Cool Breeze to the Table
Dressed Greens...................... 128
Deep-fried Chicken with Aojiso
    128
Miso Soup of Corbiculae......... 128
Ume Rice 128
Wax Gourd and Shrimp 129

The Evening Meal in Summer
Grilled Eggplants 131
Sweetened Squash 131
Sea Bass 131
Miso Soup of String Beans and
    Myoga 131

Summer Dishes in Small Bowls
Dressed Summer Vegetable
    Cubes 132
Bonito Flakes in Green Peppers
    132
Vinegared Pickling Melon 132
Chilled Tofu 133
Mountain Yam with Ume
    Flesh................................. 133
String Beans Wrapped in
    Shiso 133

AUTUMN MENUS

Appreciate the Harvest Season
Matsutake Mushrooms in a
    Teapot............................... 136
Shungiku with Walnut Dressing
    136
Mountain Yam Rolled in Beef   137
Chestnut Rice 137

Delicious and Tasteful Dishes
Simmered Saury 139
Japanese-style Salad.............. 139
Miso Soup of Assorted
    Vegetables.......................... 139

Autumn Dishes in Small Bowls
Quickly Pickled Eggplants...... 140
Kiku-nori with Citrus Fruit 140
Stir-fried Shirataki and Enoki
    Mushrooms......................... 140
Mushrooms with Cod Roe 141
Shungiku and Kamaboko with
    Lemon Soy Sauce................ 141
Kimpira of Lotus Root and
    Celery 141

WINTER MENUS

Bring Winter Scenery to the Table
Spinach with Sesame
    Dressing 144
Simmered Flounder with Roe   144
Oysters with Mizore-zu........... 145
Tofu and Vegetable Soup........ 145

The Pleasures of Cooking
One-pot Dishes
Seafood, Meat and
    Vegetable Pot 147
Turnips with Sweetened
    Vinegar 147

Winter Dishes in Small Bowls
Fruits Dressed with Grated
    Daikon............................... 148
Vinegared Dried Daikon Strips
    148
Taro and Lotus Root with
    Nanban-zu 148
Tosa-ni of Burdock................. 149
Isobe-ae of Boiled Spinach 149
Instant Pickle of Chinese
    Cabbage............................. 149

■Reconstitution of Dry Goods 35
Dried Shiitake / Freeze-dried
Tofu /Zenmai /Dried Wakame
/ Kampyo / Harusame
■Delicious Soups Depend on
Dashi Stock 108
■Unique Ingredients 115
Kiku-nori /Yuri-ne /Ginkgo Nuts
/ Suizenji-nori / Bakudaikai
■Daily Menus 121
■Table Settings 129
■How to Eat Dobin-mushi 136
■Manners for Eating Japanese
Foods 144
■Each Container has its Own
Front View 150
■Garnishes........................... 152
Sudori-shoga/Kinome/Hari-yuzu
/Musubi-Mitsuba /Momiji-oroshi
■Decorative Cuts 153
Snake's Eye / Peels of Yuzu
Citron / Cut-out Patterns /
Twisted Ume Blossom /
Cucumber Stand
■Preparation of Seafood 154
Two-piece Cut and Three-
piece Cut / Squid / Shrimp /
Shellfish
■Basic Stock and Dressings 157

Measurements used in this book:
1cup=200ml
1Tbsp(tablespoon)=15ml
1tsp(teaspoon)=5ml

Sake, mirin and dashi stock are essential to Japanese cooking.
▶Sake(rice wine)mellows food, tones down raw taste or smells and improves flavor.Dry sherry can be a substitute for sake.
▶Mirin(sweet cooking rice wine)is used to improve flavor and give food glaze and sweetness. Mirin may be substituted with 1 Tbsp sake and 1 tsp sugar.
  Both sake and mirin are now manufactured in the USA.
▶For preparations of dashi stock, see page 108.

KITCHEN EQUIPMENT PART 1

● CUTTING TOOLS

KNIVES (Hocho)

Gyuto
(Cook's knife)

Deba-bocho (Cleaver)

Sashimi-bocho
(Fish knife)

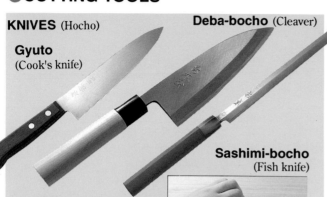

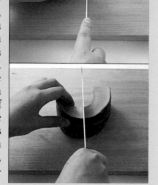

A gyuto with a blade 7" (18 cm) long is an all-purpose knife for general cutting, slicing and chopping. If possible, include in your collection a deba-bocho for cutting fish with bones and meat and a sashimi-bocho for slicing fish. In using the knife, grasp the handle with a forefinger on the back. Bend the fingers of the other hand so that the first joint of the fingers rests against the flat of the knife. In the case of hard ingredients, grasp the handle with all fingers.

CUTTING BOARD (Manaita)

Prepare a cutting board of a hinoki or Japanese cypress, 12" (30 cm) wide and 20~24"(50~60 cm) long. If you use one side for vegetables, use the other side for meat and fish. Wet the surface with water before using. When cutting strong-smelling ingredients like garlic or hard foods like ginkgo nuts, you can use the lid of a cake box or a wooden board of kamaboko (steamed fish-paste cake) instead.

● TOOLS USED WITH HEAT

JAPANESE SAUCEPAN (Yukihira-nabe)
WOODEN LID (Ki-buta)

Diameters: 6"(15 cm), 7"(18 cm), 8 1/4" (21 cm), 9 1/2" (24 cm)
Prepare four kinds of aluminum pans for Japanese cooking. Use the pans according to the ingredient to cook and the quantity: 9 1/2" pan for boiling large quantities of foods, 8" and 7" pans for cooking foods and making soup and stock, and 6" pan for a small amount of ingredients. The lid should be a little smaller than the pan and it is usually moistened with water and placed directly on the food.
(In this book, hereafter mentioned as Japanese pan.)

FLAT PAN (Hira-nabe)

A large pan of anodized aluminum. It is useful when cooking a whole fish like a flatfish.

GRILL AND IRON FRAME
(Yaki-ami and Tekkyu)

Used to grill fish. If you place a flame deflector over fire, you can easily adjust the heat and cook as if over a charcoal fire. The iron frame keeps foods at a distance from the fire and they are properly heated.

FRYING PAN (Furai-pan)

Used for broiling and stir-frying. Choose a heavy iron pan with a diameter of 9 1/2"(24 cm).

OMELET PAN (Tamagoyaki-ki)

Indispensable for cooking a thick omelet. Choose a copper pan, 7" (18 cm) by 7" (18 cm), which conducts heat well.

DEEP-FRY PAN
(Tempura-nabe)

Deep-frying requires plenty of oil, so use a large and deep pan. The oil in a shallow pan will easily catch fire. A copper pan will be best, since it conducts heat well.

STEAMER (Mushi-ki)

There are various kinds of steamers available, but a double steamer is very convenient.

EARTHENWARE CASSEROLE (Do-nabe)

An asset in the kitchen for one-pot dishes. It spreads the heat gently and evenly and the dishes stay warm for a long time after being removed from the heat. The bottom should be dry before cooking on top of the stove, or it will crack.

KITCHEN EQUIPMENT

PART 2

●OTHER USEFUL EQUIPMENT

BAMBOO DRAINER (Bon-zaru)

Prepare 2 or 3, large and small ones. Used for draining cooked ingredients and salting fish slices.

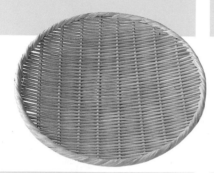

BAMBOO BASKET (Me-zaru)

It drains water well. Used for rinsing shellfish, shaking the basket.

BOWLS (Booru)

Used for washing and dressing foods. Some are made of heat-resistant glass or stainless-steel. Enamel bowls are also available. Prepare several bowls with diameters, 4 3/4~11" (12 ~ 28 cm).

FLAT CONTAINER (Batto)

Prepare 2 or 3 stainless or enamel flat container. Used for seasoning ingredients and coating foods. Together with wire netting, it is convenient to drain fried foods.

FINE SIEVES (Uragoshi-ki)

Used for making dressings and straining boiled eggs. The best mesh is made of horse hair. When using, slant the strainer.

MORTAR AND PESTLE
(Suribachi and Surikogi)

Used for grinding sesame seeds and blending ingredients. Choose a mortar with a diameter of 9 1/2" (24 cm). The best pestle is made of a prickly ash.

SCALE (Hakari)

Choose a scale, which is graduated in every 3/16 oz (5 g). It should weigh 35 oz (1 kg).

MEASURING CUP AND SPOONS (Keiryo kappu and supuun)

It is important to measure ingredients correctly. One cup measures 200ml. A tablespoon measures 15ml and a teaspoon 5ml. All should be leveled off. Powders like sugar and salt are leveled with a spoon handle.

BAMBOO MAT (Makisu)

Prepare two different sizes of mats, 12 3/8×12" (31×30 cm) for thick sushi rolls and 8×9 1/2" (20×24 cm) for omelets. Wash well and dry completely after use.

NET SCOOP (Ami-jakushi)

Used for scooping up the impurities after foods are deep-fried and small fish after cooked.

WOODEN TUB (Handai)

Used for making sushi rice and evaporating excess moisture from rice dishes. Get a tub of Japanese cypress with a diameter of 14 1/4" (36 cm).

BRUSH (Hake)

Used for brushing sauce and batter evenly over the surface of ingredients.

COOKING CHOPSTICKS (Sai-bashi)

Get 3 or 4 sets of bamboo chopsticks, long and short. Long chopsticks for deep-frying and boiling ingredients. Short ones for simmered foods and serving.

OIL STRAINER (Abura-koshiki)

Used for straining the impurities from oil used for deep-frying and storing. Choose the strainer, which contains a lid of wire netting.

STRAINER (Banno-koshiki)

An all-purpose tool used for straining water and a variety of ingredients.

RICE PADDLE (Ki-jakushi)

Used for serving rice and mixing.

SCUM SCOOP (Aku-sukui)

Get a one with fine mesh.

LADLE AND PERFORATED LADLE (Tama- and Ana-jakushi)

The ladle is used for pouring liquids and the perforated ladle for draining liquids.

GRATER (Oroshi-gane)

Used for grating Japanese daikon and ginger. Sharkskin is best for wasabi or Japanese horseradish.

BAMBOO SKEWERS (Take-gushi)

Used to check cooked foods and serving small ingredients.

TWEEZERS (Hone-nuki)

Used to remove small bones from fish.

METAL SKEWERS (Kana-gushi)

Prepare five skewers per set (long and short) for grilling fish.

BASIC CUTTING TECHNIQUES

The same vegetables require different cooking methods and seasoning according to the way they are cut.

Therefore it is important to adopt the appropriate cutting techniques. The beautiful arrangements of food on a plate depend on the cutting, so cut ingredients with care and attention keeping the result in mind.

Butsu-giri (Chunks)

Cut slender cylindrical vegetables like naganegi and burdocks in appropriate uniform lengths. Use the first piece to measure.

Naname-giri (Diagonal cuts)

Cut slender cylindrical vegetables like naganegi and cucumbers diagonally from one end.

Wa-giri (Rounds)

Slice cylindrical vegetables crosswise into rounds of uniform thickness appropriate for the recipe.

Sogi-giri (Slanting cuts)

Cut thick vegetables into thin slices with a knife slightly slanted. Food sliced in this way is easily seasoned.

Hangetsu-giri (Half-moons)

Cut cylindrical vegetables in half lengthwise, and place with the cut face down. Slice crosswise into half-moons.

Kushigata-giri (Wedge cuts)

Cut round vegetables like tomatoes and onions in half and into uniform wedges.

Icho-giri (Quarter-rounds)

Cut cylindrical vegetables in quarters lengthwise. Slice crosswise into quarter-rounds of uniform thickness.

Zaku-giri (Large cuts)

Cut leaves like cabbages and Chinese cabbages into large pieces. "Zaku-zaku" stands for the cutting sounds.

Ran-giri (Rolling wedges)

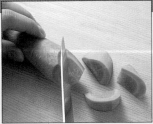

Cut cylindrical vegetables diagonally into uniform pieces, while rotating. The seasoning is well absorbed through the many surfaces.

Cut diagonally into bite-sized pieces, rotating towards you.

In case of big cylindrical vegetables like daikon radishes, cut in half lengthwise in advance. Cut into quarters lengthwise and cut diagonally, rotating.

Tanzaku-giri (Rectangles)

Cut vegetables into thin rectangles, 1 1/2~2" (4~5 cm) long and 3/8" (1 cm) thick.

Cut into pieces, 1 1/2~2" (4~5 cm) wide.

Discard the curved four sides and cut the rest into thin slabs, 3/8" (1 cm) thick.

Cut into the same thicknesses.

Hyoshigi-giri (Sticks)

Cut vegetables into thin sticks, 1 1/2~2" (4~5 cm) long and 1/4~3/8" (5~10 mm) thick.

Cut into a rectangular block, discarding curved sides.

Slice into rectangles, 1/4~3/8" (5~10 mm) thick.

Cut into sticks, 1/4~3/8" (5~10 mm) thick.

Sainome-giri (Dice cuts)

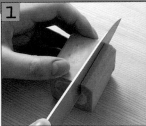

Cut rectangular sticks into 3/8" (1 cm) dices.

Slice rectangular blocks, 1 1/2~2" (4~5 cm) long, into slabs, 3/8" (1 cm) thick.

Cut into sticks, 3/8" (1 cm) thick, along the grain.

Align sticks together and cut into 3/8" (1 cm) dices.

Sen-giri (Julienne strips)

Cut vegetables into thin strips, 1 1/2~2" (4~5cm) long with the grain running in the same direction as the cut.

Discard the curved side and place the cut-side down to settle.

Cut into thin slices along the grain.

Stack the slices, overlapping slightly, and cut into thin strips.

Koguchi-giri (Edge cuts)

Starting from one end, cut slender cylindrical vegetables like cucumbers and naganegi into thin uniform round slices according to recipes.

1 For cucumbers, cut the top end off.

2 Peel the skin 3/4 " (2 cm) from the end, because it is hard and bitter to taste.

3 Slice a little inward with the top of a knife so that the slices do not roll.

Mijin-giri (Mincing) <Onion>

Cut up vegetables into very small pieces. In the case of onions, make cuts crisscross in advance.

1 Cut in half lengthwise, and make thin vertical cuts taking care not cut through.

2 Make the same horizontal 2 or 3 cuts.

3 Holding tightly with one hand, cut up into very fine pieces from one end.

Mijin-giri (Mincing) <Naganegi>

Make shallow cuts lengthwise in advance to get finely chopped pieces.

1 Rolling the naganegi, make lengthwise cuts with the top of a knife.

2 Hold the strips together, and mince finely from one end.

<Ginger>

In the case of vegetables like ginger and garlic, cut into fine strips in advance, then mince.

Sasagaki (Shaving cuts)

Shave slender vegetables like burdock thinly into the shape of bamboo leaves with a knife as if sharpening a stick.

1 Make shallow cuts lengthwise with the top of a knife.

2 Place horizontally on a cutting board and shave, rolling as if sharpening a pencil.

3 Soak immediately in vinegared water and culinary bleach until the water becomes brown.

Shiraga-negi cuts (Julienne strips)

Cut vegetables like naganegi (Japanese bunching onion) into thin strips along the grain. It looks like shiraga (white hair).

1 Cut into pieces, 1 1/2~2" (4~5 cm) long and make a cut lengthwise as far as the middle.

2 Open the cut and discard the slim core.

3 Place the inside down and cut into thin strips from one end.

SIMMERED DISHES

Nimono

BRAISED CHICKEN

Iri-dori

Stir-fried chicken and vegetables are braised in strongly seasoned liquid. This dish is called 'Chikuzen-ni' at Hakata in Kyushu and is served on the occasion of a festival and in the New Year.

TIPS

1. Remove excess oil from ingredients in boiled water before simmering.
2. Taros cooked over low heat are liable to fall to pieces, so cook over rather high heat.

INGREDIENTS

7 oz (200 g) chicken thigh
16 oz (450 g) taros
1 3/4 oz (50 g) carrot
1 3/4 oz (50 g) burdock
3 1/2 oz (100 g) lotus root
1/2 konnyaku (devil's tongue jelly)
6 small dried shiitake mushrooms
15 snow peas
1 1/2 Tbsp salad oil

Simmering stock

1 1/2 cups dashi stock or water / 2 Tbsp sake / 3 Tbsp sugar / 1 1/2 Tbsp mirin / 3 Tbsp soy sauce

PREPARATION

■Taros

①Brush and wash mud away from taros. Cut both ends off.
②Peel the skin to make six sides. Cut in halves and soak immediately in water. Wash briefly.
③Cover with water and 1/2 tsp salt in a small pan and bring to a boil.
④When it comes to a boil, discard water and wash under running water. Boil again in water without salt two times and remove sliminess.

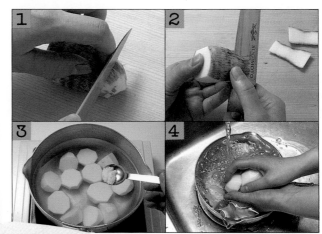

TO SERVE

Arrange ingredients with color in mind. Place green snow peas here and there for accents.

■Chicken

Remove and discard the yellow fat and skin sticking out of the body. Cut lengthwise in half and into bite-sized pieces.

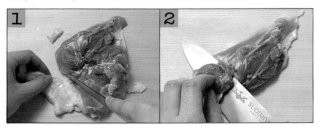

■Carrot, Burdock, Lotus root

Carrot: Peel skin and cut into bite-sized pieces. Soak in water.
Burdock: Brush in water and cut into bite-sized pieces. Soak in vinegared water until water turns brown to remove harshness. Rinse and drain in a colander.
Lotus root: Peel skin and cut into bite-sized pieces. Soak in vinegared water for 3~4 minutes. Rinse and drain.

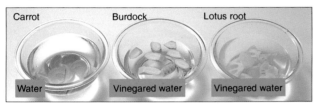

■Konnyaku

Place in water and bring to a boil. Boil for 5 minutes and transfer to cold water. Cut into bite-sized pieces with a spoon.

■Dried shiitake mushrooms

Wash briefly and soak in water until soft. Place a weight like a plate on them to prevent from floating. Cut stems off.

■Snow peas

Remove strings and parboil briefly in salted water.

METHOD
Japanese pan, 8 1/4"(21 cm)

1. Stir-fry chicken and vegetables.

Heat 1/2 Tbsp salad oil in a pan. Remove the pan from heat and let it cool placed on a wet cloth. Add the chicken and coat with the oil. Stir-fry over medium heat until slightly colored and transfer to a bamboo colander. Heat the rest of the oil in the pan. Stir-fry all the other ingredients except snow peas. Transfer all to the same colander.

Medium heat

2. Remove excess oil.

Pour plenty of boiling water over to remove excess oil. (*Abura-nuki, see footnote). This will improve the taste and prevent the oil from coming out on the surface when cooled.

3. Simmer until the liquid has almost evaporated.

Add all the ingredients in a pan with the dashi stock and stock ingredients. Simmer over high heat. When it comes to a boil, turn heat to medium. Skim off any scums that forms and continue simmering with a wooden lid dropped directly onto the food. In the meantime, turn the ingredients upside down (nabe-gaeshi, p. 17). When the liquid is almost reduced, slant the pan and boil down the liquid. Transfer to a metal pan.

High heat

Medium heat

*Abura-nuki: The method is to pour boiling water over oily ingredients to remove oil from the surface. It gets rid of the smell of oil and improves the taste.

BRAISED BEEF AND POTATOES

Niku-jaga

One of the most popular Japanese dishes. The taste of this home cooking is especially relished by men. Use dry textured potatoes and fatty meat.

TIPS

1. Heat the oil and cool it before sautéing the beef.
2. Cook until the liquid is reduced. Transfer to a flat container to cool.

INGREDIENTS

7 oz (200 g) sliced beef
14 oz (400 g) potatoes
7 oz (200 g) onion
1/2 Tbsp salad oil

Simmering stock
2 cups dashi stock or water / 3 Tbsp sake / 3 Tbsp sugar /
2 Tbsp mirin / 3 Tbsp soy sauce

TO SERVE

Place the ingredients in a heap. It looks beautiful.

PREPARATION

Cut the potatoes before peeling.

■Potato

The easy way to peel the potatoes is to cut them in advance.
①Brush under running water washing mud away.
②Remove the eyes (see footnote) and spoiled parts with the edge of a knife.
③Cut into 8 portions, a little larger than bite-sized pieces.
④Peel and soak immediately in water. Wash briefly and drain in a colander.

■Sliced beef

Place 2 or 3 slices together and cut into bite-sized pieces. Separate the pieces.

■Onion

Peel and cut in half lengthwise. Remove the heart and place cut-side down. Cut into slices, 3/8" (1 cm) wide.

*Potato eyes:They contain toxic substances, so you must remove them before cooking.

METHOD

1. Heat pan and cool before sautéing beef.

Heat the oil in a pan. Remove from heat to a wet dishcloth and cool it to prevent the beef from sticking to the bottom. Add the beef and coat with oil, separating with chopsticks. Return the pan to moderate heat and brown the beef, stirring.

Medium heat

2. Sauté together with vegetables.

When the beef changes color, add the onion and potatoes. Sauté, stirring with a wooden spatula.

3. Add the dashi stock and season.

Add just enough dashi stock or water to cover the ingredients. Bring to a boil over high heat, skimming off any scum that forms. Add the sake, sugar, mirin and soy sauce in this order.

High heat

4. Skim off scum again and cover with a drop lid.

Lower the heat slightly and bring the mixture to a boil. Skim off remaining scum and cover with a moistened drop lid.

Slightly high heat

5. Flip the ingredients over when the liquid is reduced to one-third.

Hold the handles of the pan with both hands (beginners can hold one handle and the edge of the pan) and shake it, turning the ingredients upside down to coat evenly.

(nabe-gaeshi).

6. Boil down the liquid and transfer to a flat container.

Braise over high heat, slanting the pan until the liquid has been absorbed. Transfer to a flat container and spread. When cooled, savory niku-jaga is completed.

High heat

17

ASSORTMENT OF SIMMERED FOODS
Taki-awase

Taki-awase is an assortment of foods, each of which is cooked using different methods and served together. Relish the tastes of a salty butterbur and slightly sweet tofu and shiitake.

TIPS

1. Simmer freeze-dried tofu and shiitake until they absorb the liquid.
2. Cook butterbur briefly and season with the simmering stock.

INGREDIENTS

1 freeze-dried tofu
4 dried shiitake mushrooms
4 stalks butterbur, each 8" (20 cm)
6 shrimp

Dried wakame
Kinome
(young leaves of prickly ash)

Simmering stock

■Freeze-dried tofu
1 cup dashi stock / 1 Tbsp sake / 1 Tbsp sugar / 1/2 Tbsp mirin / 1/2 Tbsp light soy sauce / Dash salt

■Dried shiitake mushroom
1/2 cup dashi stock / 1/2 Tbsp sugar / 1 Tbsp mirin / 1/2 Tbsp soy sauce

■Butterbur
1 cup dashi stock / 1/2 Tbsp sake / 2/3 Tbsp light soy sauce / 1/3 tsp salt

---

PREPARATION
Parboil butterbur and shrimp. Soak tofu and shiitake in water.

■Butterbur
Wash briefly in water. Place on a cutting board, sprinkle with salt and roll with both hands. (*Ita-zuri)

Add the salted butterbur to plenty of boiling water and parboil for 1 minute.

Transfer to cold water immediately and let stand until cool.

Remove the skins and fibrous outer veins. First peel the end a little and then pull all the way.

■Freeze-dried tofu
Soak in lukewarm water to soften. Wash under running water well and squeeze water out (see p. 35).

■Shrimp
Devein with a bamboo skewer. Parboil in salted water and cool in a colander. Remove head and tail and peel the shell from the body.

■Dried shiitake mushroom
Choose smaller shiitake. Wash briefly and soak in plenty of water to soften. Squeeze water out and cut off the stems.

■Dried wakeme
Soak in water for about 5 minutes. Remove stalks and cut in bite-sized pieces. Parboil and soak in water and drain.

---

*Ita-zuri: Preparation to bring out the color of vegetables such as butterbur and cucumber. Sprinkle salt over the ingredients and roll on a cutting board with both hands.

1. Freeze-dried tofu.

Bring the simmering stock to a boil in a 6"(15 cm) pan and add tofu. Cover with a paper lid and simmer gently over medium heat until the liquid is reduced. Press the tofu with a wooden lid to squeeze out the liquid. Continue to heat for a while. Repeat this 2 or 3 times until the liquid is gone. Transfer to a flat container.

Medium low heat

2. Shiitake mushrooms.

Bring the simmering stock to a boil in a 6"(15 cm) pan. Add the shiitake and sugar and cook for 3 to 4 minutes. Add mirin and soy sauce and simmer over low heat covered with an aluminum lid until the liquid is almost reduced. Slant the pan and boil over high heat until the liquid is gone. Transfer to a flat container.

Low heat

High heat

3. Butterbur.

Bring the simmering stock to a boil in an 8 1/4" (21 cm) pan. Add the butterbur and bring to a boil again. Separate the butterbur and the liquid and fan to cool. When the liquid has been cooled completely, soak the butterbur to flavor.

High heat

4. Soak shrimp and wakame in the butterbur liquid.

Separate half the amount of the liquid in which the butterbur is cooked and soak shrimp and wakame in it for 4 to 5 minutes.

TO SERVE

Cut the tofu in half lengthwise and then slice like stairs. Quarter the butterbur. Place vegetables in the back and seafood in the front. Garnish with the kinome.

FLATFISH COOKED QUICKLY

Karei no haya-ni

For fresh flatfish, 'Quick cooking' is recommended. The method is to cook the whole fish quickly and season lightly. The plain taste of the white meat is the focus of this cooking.

INGREDIENTS

2 whole flatfish, about 10 1/2 oz (300 g) each
Komatsuna (a kind of Chinese cabbage)

Simmering stock
2 cups dashi stock / 3 Tbsp sake / 1 Tbsp sugar / 2 Tbsp mirin /
2 1/2 Tbsp soy sauce

TIPS

1. Carefully remove the slime of dorsal and pelvic fins and the tail.
2. Continue to baste with simmering stock.

TO SERVE

Contrary to ordinary fish, place the head of the fish on the right. Spread the liquid and put the komatsuna in the front.

PREPARATION

It is very important to remove slime from the flatfish.

1. Remove slime.

The dorsal and pelvic fins and tail have slime with a muddy smell. Scrape it off with a knife. The tail has lots of slime, so carefully remove it.

2. Remove scales.

Lay the fish with the black skin upward and the head on the left. Lift the head a little with one hand and scrape off the fish scales from the tail toward the head with a knife.

3. Remove gills.

Place the head on the right. Insert the knife under the gill opening and detach the base of the gill cover, drawing the red part out.

4. Remove guts.

Make a cut about 2" (5 cm) below the pectoral fins on the white skin. Turn it over, push the back of the cut and draw the guts out with a knife.

5. Rinse under running water.

Remove the remaining guts with fingers under running water. Rinse quickly and pat dry completely.

6. Make cuts on the skin.

Make about five cuts crosswise diagonally at intervals of 3/4" (2 cm) (*Nimono-bocho). Move the knife toward you.

*Nimono-bocho:
Cuts made on the fish skin so as to cook well and prevent the skin from breaking. There are a variety of cutting methods, crosswise diagonals and cross strips, etc.

1. Bring the simmering stock to a boil.

Add the dashi stock to the pan and bring it to a boil over high heat. When it comes to a boil, add the ingredients for the simmering stock and bring it to a boil again.

2. Baste with simmering stock.

Place fish with the black skin upward and baste with simmering stock with a ladle to prevent the fish from breaking into pieces. When the color of the surface with cuts has changed, do the same with another fish.

3. Cover with a drop lid of aluminum foil.

Turn the heat to medium and cover the fish with aluminum foil as a drop lid. Avoid using a wooden drop lid, or the heavy weight will spoil the skin of the fish.

4. Simmer for 5~6 minutes.

Simmer for 5~6 minutes and turn off the heat. Boil the komatsuna briefly in salted water, cut into pieces, soak in the liquid and garnish.

SIMMERED KINMEDAI (Alfonsino)
Kinmedai no nitsuke

The best season to savor kinmedai is winter, when it puts on fat. It is rather strongly seasoned. It is served hot, so do not start simmering until everything is ready at the table.

TIP
Add the fish to boiling stock and adjust the heat.

INGREDIENTS

2 fillets kinmedai, each 3 1/2 oz (100 g)
1/2 pack kaiwarena (daikon radish sprouts)

Simmering stock
3/4 cups dashi stock / 2 Tbsp sake / 1 1/2 Tbsp sugar /
1 1/2 Tbsp mirin / 1 1/2 Tbsp soy sauce

PREPARATION

■**Kinmedai**
If the fish is moist, pat dry. Score slits crosswise on the skin to heat through.

■**Kaiwarena**
Parboil for a short time.

METHOD
Japanese pan, 7" (18 cm)

1. Add to boiling stock with the skin side up.

Bring the dashi stock to a boil over high heat. Add seasoning ingredients and bring to a boil again. Add the fish with the skin side up. (*see footnote). Do not add before coming to a boil or the fishy smell will remain.

High heat

2. Pour the stock over.

Baste the fish with stock 3~4 times with a ladle to make the meat firm.

3. Cover with a drop-lid.

Cover with a lid of aluminum foil directly over the fish. Simmer for 7~8 minutes over medium heat so that the stock just covers the fish.

Medium heat

4. The cooked fish.

TO SERVE
Arrange the fish with the skin side up. Dip the kaiware-na in the stock and place in front of the fish. Pour the stock over the whole.

*The skin side up: When simmering fish fillets, always place the skin side up or the skin sticks to the pan.

SIMMERED MACKEREL IN MISO
Saba no miso-ni

TIPS

1. Add ginger to reduce fishy odor.
2. Add miso last to preserve its aroma.

INGREDIENTS

1/2 fillet mackerel, 10 1/2 oz (300 g)
1/2 naganegi (Japanese bunching onion)
1 clove ginger
2 Tbsp hatcho-miso (dark and salty miso)

Simmering stock
1/2 cup dashi stock / 2 Tbsp sake / 2 Tbsp sugar / 2 Tbsp mirin /
1 Tbsp soy sauce

PREPARATION

■Mackerel
Cut into 3 fillets as shown on page 154. Place on a cutting board with the skin side down. Cut the fillet diagonally into 4~6 pieces.

■Naganegi, Ginger
Grill naganegi over the fire until browned in places. Cut into 1 1/4" (3 cm) lengths. Cut the ginger into thin slices.

METHOD   Japanese pan, 7" (18 cm)

1. Simmer in stock with sake and sugar.

Bring the dashi stock to a boil over high heat. Add seasonings and ginger. Place the fish with skin side up. Cover with an aluminum drop-lid and cook over medium heat for 2~3 minutes.

High heat

2. Add the mirin and soy sauce.

After the fish is well seasoned, add the mirin and soy sauce. Cover with an aluminum lid again and continue cooking for another 2~3 minutes.

Medium heat

3. Dissolve the miso in simmering stock.

Turn off the heat. Dissolve the miso in simmering stock. Cook again over medium heat.

4. Shake the pan and boil down.

The miso makes the fish liable to scorch, so shake the pan while cooking for 1~2 minutes until the liquid is reduced.

TO SERVE
Arrange the fish on a plate. Dip the naganegi in the simmering stock and place in front. Pour the stock over.

*Miso: Use thick and strong miso such as hatcho-miso and sendai-miso.

SIMMERED PORK WITH DAIKON RADISH
Buta-baraniku to daikon no nimono

TIP

Light seasoning is the point, since the simmering stock is also eaten.

INGREDIENTS

5 1/4 oz (150 g) boneless pork belly
14 oz (400 g) daikon radish
3 1/2 oz (100 g) carrot
5~6 small fresh shiitake mushrooms
Daikon radish leaves
1 Tbsp vegetable oil

Simmering stock

3 cups dashi stock / 2 1/2 Tbsp sake / 1 tsp salt /
1 Tbsp light soy sauce

PREPARATION

■Pork belly
Cut into pieces, 3/8" (1 cm) wide. Cut the pieces, 3/4" (2 cm) wide at a right angle to the fat.

■Daikon radish, Carrot
Daikon: Peel and quarter lengthwise. Cut into the bite-sized pieces diagonally, rotating (rangiri). Soak in water immediately after cutting and drain in a colander.
Carrot: Peel and cut into pieces, a little smaller than the daikon radish.

■Shiitake mushrooms
Wipe the caps with a wet dishtowel. Cut off the stems.

■Daikon radish leaves
Use inside thin leaves. Parboil in salted water and soak in chilled water. Squeeze out the water and chop finely.

METHOD　　Japanese pan, 8 1/4" (21 cm)

1. Heat and cool a pan before adding the pork.

Heat the oil in a pan. Remove from the heat and cool on a dampened dishtowel to prevent the pork from sticking to the bottom. Add the pork and coat with oil, separating with chopsticks. Return the pan to the heat and stir-fry over medium heat until browned.

2. Stir-fry together with vegetables.

Add the daikon and carrot. Stir-fry until the corners of daikon become translucent. Add mushrooms and stir-fry together quickly.

High heat

3. Add the dashi stock and skim off any scum.

Pour the dashi stock over to cover. Bring to a boil, skimming off any scum that forms.

High heat

*Summer daikon and winter daikon: Summer daikon is good for grating and salad, and winter daikon for simmering.

4. Add seasonings and cover with a drop-lid.

Turn the heat to medium and add the sake, salt and light soy sauce in this order. Cover with a wet drop-lid and simmer.

Medium heat

5. Test doneness with a bamboo skewer.

Continue to simmer for 15 minutes. If a bamboo skewer easily pierces through the daikon, everything is done.

TO SERVE
Transfer to a deep bowl and cover with plenty of simmering stock. Scatter chopped daikon leaves over.

SIMMERED TURNIPS WITH MINCED CHICKEN

Kabu no soboro-ni

TIPS

1. Cook the chicken quickly and crumble.
2. Bring the cornstarch mixture to a boil to get rid of the flour odor.

INGREDIENTS

6 turnips, each 3 1/2 oz (100g)
5 1/4 oz (150 g) minced chicken
1/2 Tbsp vegetable oil
1/2 Tbsp cornstarch
1 Tbsp ginger juice
Yuzu citron peel

Simmering stock

1 1/2 cups dashi stock / 2 Tbsp sake / 2 Tbsp sugar /
1 Tbsp mirin / 2 Tbsp light soy sauce

TO SERVE

Arrange the turnips and chicken in a bowl together with the cooked stock. Top with yuzu peel.

PREPARATION

■Turnips

①Cut off leaves, leaving about 3/4" (2 cm) of stalks. Place the head out of the cutting board to let the stalks intact.
②Wash dirt from the base of the stalks under running water with a bamboo skewer.
③Make shallow cuts around stalks to make it easy to peel.
④Peel from the bottom upwards. Cut in half lengthwise. Wash briefly and drain.

■Minced chicken

Remove the skin and fat, if possible. Use the chicken ground twice.

■Yuzu citorn peel

Cut into fine strips. See 'hari-yuzu' on page 152.

METHOD
Japanese pan, 8 1/4"(21 cm)

1. Cook minced chicken first.

Bring the dashi stock to a boil and add seasonings and minced chicken. Stir with several cooking chopsticks to prevent from sticking together.

High heat

2. Cook turnips until soft.

Turn the heat to medium. Skim the surface to remove foam. Add the turnips and cover with a wet drop-lid. Cook for 10 minutes until a bamboo skewer easily pierce through.

Medium heat

3. Thicken the stock and add flavor.

Slant the pan to collect the stock. Add cornstarch dissolved in 1 Tbsp water. Bring to a boil to thicken the stock, shaking the pan. Add the ginger juice to taste.

*Ingredients good for this dish: Daikon radish, taro, wax gourd, eggplant and Chinese cabbage.

KAMABOKO AND MITSUBA COOKED WITH EGGS

Kamaboko to mitsuba no tamago-toji

TIP

Turn off the heat when eggs are half-cooked.

INGREDIENTS

1/4 slice kamaboko (steamed fish-paste cake)
Carrot
1 small bunch mitsuba (honewort)
2 eggs

Simmering stock

1 cup dashi stock / 1 Tbsp sake / 1 tsp sugar / 1 tsp mirin /
1/2 Tbsp light soy sauce

PREPARATION

■Carrot
Cut into julienne strips the same length as the kamaboko.

■Mitsuba
Wash briefly in water and drain. Cut into 3/4" (2 cm) lengths.

■Eggs
Break eggs in a bowl. Use cooking chopsticks to lift up the egg whites 3 or 4 times. Beat lightly.

■Kamaboko
Cut into thin slices diagonally. Pile the slices, overlapping slightly and cut into julienne strips (sen-giri on p. 11).

METHOD

Japanese pan, 7" (18 cm)

1. Cook the carrot and kamaboko.

Bring the dashi stock to a boil in a pan and add seasonings. Add the carrot and kamaboko in this order over medium heat and bring each to a boil.

Medium heat

2. Add the mitsuba and egg mixture. Cover with a lid.

Scatter the mitsuba and pour over the egg mixture by using chopsticks to guide it. Turn off the heat. Cover with a lid and allow to stand for a while until the eggs are half-cooked.

TO SERVE

Transfer the whole to a serving plate. Use a container with a lid, if available.

NABE-SHIGI OF EGGPLANT

Nasu no nabe-shigi

Nabe-shigi is vegetables stir-fried in oil and glazed with miso. Sesame oil is recommended.

TIPS

1. Use plenty of oil because eggplants absorb oil well.
2. Add the miso last and cook over high heat.

PREPARATION

■String beans

Remove strings. Snap each bean into 3 equal parts instead of using a knife.

■Eggplants

①Cut off the end and cut in half lengthwise.
②Cut in half crossways and then cut into 1/8" (3~4 mm) thick pieces.
③Soak in water immediately to remove harshness and prevent from discoloring.
④Allow to stand for 2~3 minutes and drain. Pat dry with a kitchen towel.

INGREDIENTS

3 eggplants, each 3 1/2 oz (100 g)
3 1/2 oz (100 g) string beans
3 Tbsp sesame oil
1 Tbsp hatcho-miso (dark and salty miso)
Shichimi-togarashi (seven-spice pepper)

Simmering stock

1/2 cup dashi stock / 3 Tbsp sake / 2 Tbsp sugar / 1 Tbsp mirin / 1 Tbsp soy sauce

METHOD — Japanese pan, 8 1/4" (21 cm)

1. Stir-fry eggplants and string beans.

Heat the oil in a pan and stir-fry eggplants quickly over medium heat. When they become tender, add string beans and stir-fry together briefly until they are coated with oil.

Medium heat

2. Add the simmering stock and cook until reduced to half.

Pour the simmering stock over and add seasonings. Stir with chopsticks and continue to cook for 3~4 minutes until the liquid has been reduced to half.

3. Add the miso and cook until the liquid is almost gone.

Slant the pan and collect the ingredients at one side. Add the miso and dissolve with chopsticks. Cook over high heat, combining the whole, until the liquid is almost gone.

TO SERVE

Transfer to a flat container to cool. Serve piled in bowls and sprinkle with shichimi-togarashi or powdered Japanese pepper as desired.

*Ingredients good for this dish: Summer vegetables such as green pepper, sweet green pepper, etc. Chicken thigh can be also added.

BURDOCK KIMPIRA

Kimpira-gobo

Cook quickly over high heat to make crisp kimpira. For elderly people, add 3 Tbsp dashi stock to make it tender.

TIPS

1. To retain the flavor, don't scrape away the skin of burdock.
2. The liquid must completely be reduced to finish.

INGREDIENTS

3 1/2 oz (100 g) burdock root
1 red chili pepper
1 Tbsp vegetable oil

Simmering stock

3 Tbsp sake / 1 Tbsp sugar / 1 Tbsp mirin / 1 Tbsp soy sauce

PREPARATION

■**Burdock**
①Scrub with a brush under running water. The skin has the flavor, so be sure not to scrape it off.
②Cut into pieces 1 1/2"(4 cm) long and soak in water with a little vinegar added. Cut each piece lengthwise into thin slices and soak again immediately in vinegared water.
③When the color of the water changes to brown and the harshness is removed, rinse in water and drain in a colander.

■**Red chili pepper**
Soak in lukewarm water for 2 minutes until soft. Cut off the end and remove seeds with a bamboo skewer. Cut into round slices.

*Ingredients good for kimpira: Udo, lotus root, carrot and celery.

METHOD   Japanese pan, 7" (18 cm)

1. Stir-fry the burdock quickly.

Heat the oil in a pan and stir-fry the burdock quickly over high heat, stirring with chopsticks. When the whole is coated with the oil, add the red chili pepper and mix well.

High heat

2. Add seasonings and continue to stir-fry.

Lower the heat to medium and gradually add seasonings. Continue to stir-fry until the liquid is reduced.

High-medium heat

3. The liquid has been completely absorbed.

Slant the pan and cook until the liquid is almost gone. Coat the whole with the liquid. Transfer to a flat container to cool. Place in a dish.

NIBITASHI OF KOMATSUNA AND ABURAGE
Komatsuna to aburage no nibitashi

Nibitashi is one of the best cooking methods to eat plenty of vegetables, which are simmered in lightly seasoned liquid.

TIPS
1. Greens should be divided into several parts to parboil so as not to be overcooked.
2. Start with the ingredient, which requires longer time for cooking.

INGREDIENTS

7 oz (200 g) komatsuna
1 sheet aburage (deep-fried tofu)

Simmering stock
1 1/2 cups dashi stock / 1 Tbsp sake / 1/2 Tbsp mirin /
2 Tbsp light soy sauce

TO SERVE
Heap in deep bowls and cover with the simmering stock.

PREPARATION

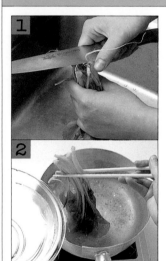

■Komatsuna
①Cut off root hairs and soak in water for a while to make it easy to remove the sand around the roots. Rinse well under running water.
②Add a dash of salt to ample boiling water. Put in from the stems one by one and then leaves. When they become soft, transfer to cold water.
③Put all the roots together in the water. Squeeze the water out.
④Trim off the root ends and cut the whole into 1 1/4" (3 cm) lengths.

■Aburage
Remove excess oil(Aburanuki,p.15). Cut in half lengthwise. Lay one on top of another and cut together into pieces, 1/4" (5 mm) wide.

METHOD   Japanese pan, 8 1/4" (21 cm)

1. Bring the dashi stock to a boil and cook the aburage.

Bring the dashi stock to a boil in a pan. Add the aburage and cook over medium heat for 1~2 minutes.

Medium heat

2. Add seasonings to taste.

Add the sake, mirin and light soy sauce in this order. Cook for another 1~2 minutes until the aburage is well seasoned.

3. Add the komatsuna last and cook quickly.

Scatter the komatsuna over. Bring to a boil and immediately turn off the heat.
If you cook longer, the komatsuna will become too soft and loses its color.

*Komatsuna: Brassica campestris (rapifera group). It is a kind of Chinese cabbage. Available throughout all seasons, but the one in winter is the best.

NIBITASHI OF CHINESE CABBAGE AND LITTLENECK CLAMS

Winter

Hakusai to asari no nibitashi

Cook the leaves and stalks of Chinese cabbage separately so that they are cooked evenly. The point is to add sugar to bring out the sweetness of the Chinese cabbage.

INGREDIENTS

10 1/2 oz (300 g) Chinese cabbage / 7 oz (200 g) littleneck clams (shelled) / 1 clove ginger
Simmering stock
1 1/2 cups dashi stock / 2 Tbsp sake / 2 Tbsp mirin / 1 tsp sugar / 2 Tbsp light soy sauce / Dash salt

PREPARATION

Chinese cabbage: Separate the leaves and stalks. Cut the leaves in half lengthwise and then cut crosswise into julienne strips. Cut the stalks lengthwise into julienne strips.
Littleneck clams: Rinse in a colander under running water.
Ginger: Peel and cut into fine strips and soak in water briefly.

METHOD
Japanese pan, 8 1/4" (21 cm)

1. Bring the dashi stock to a boil. Add the cabbage stalks and cook over medium heat.
2. Gather the cabbage stalks to one side and add the littleneck clams in the open space. (*Nabe-wari). Add seasonings and bring to a boil.
3. Gather the stalks and clams to one side. Add the cabbage leaves in the open space. Cook until tender and turn off the heat. Place the whole in a bowl and pour the liquid over. Garnish with ginger strips.

Medium heat

NIBITASHI OF LETTUCE AND YOUNG SARDINES

All seasons

Retasu to jako no nibitashi

Young sardines should be seasoned lightly, since they are salty. Cook the lettuce quickly so that it retains crispness.

INGREDIENTS

12 1/2 oz (350 g) lettuce / 1 cup young sardines
Simmering stock
1 cup dashi stock / 2 Tbsp sake / 1/2 tsp salt / 1 Tbsp light soy sauce

PREPARATION

Lettuce: Remove the core and wash under running water. Separate each leaf. Drain and tear into bite-sized pieces.
Young sardines: If salty, pour boiling water over to remove the salt.

METHOD
Japanese pan, 8 1/4" (21 cm)

1. Bring the dashi stock to a boil in a pan and add seasonings.
2. Add the lettuce and cook briefly over medium heat, turning over until tender.
3. Scatter the young sardines over and mix once and turn off the heat.

Medium heat

---

*Nabe-wari: The method to separate ingredients in a pan so that each ingredient is grouped in a dish to serve.

31

SIMMERED KIDNEY BEANS

Kintokimame no ama-ni

Use fresh beans harvested in autumn. Cooked beans give a homey atmosphere to the table.

TIPS

1. Cook over medium low heat. High heat cracks skins and low heat the beans.
2. Take care so that beans are always covered with boiling water.

INGREDIENTS

2 cups kidney beans, 10 1/2 oz (300 g)
3 cups sugar, 11 1/2 oz (330g)
1 Tbsp light soy sauce

PREPARATION

Wash the beans in a bowl under running water, rubbing with hands. Discard imperfect ones. Leave in 8 cups of water to soak overnight. Reserve the soaking water.

Before soaking   After soaking

METHOD   Japanese pan, 8 1/4" (21 cm)

1. Cook with the reserved soaking water.

Bring the beans and the reserved soaking water to a boil over high heat, skimming off any scum that forms.

High heat

2. Pour in cold water.

Pour 1/2 cup cold water (*bikkuri-mizu). When it returns to a boil, add another 1/2 cup water. Repeat this twice. Turn the heat to medium high and cover with an aluminum drop-lid.

Medium high heat

3. Test the doneness by crushing with fingers.

Cook beans for 40~60 minutes, adding water if necessary to cover. Test the doneness by crushing one bean with fingers.

4. Season and leave overnight.

Add the sugar all at one time. When dissolved, cover with an aluminum drop-lid and cook for 4~5 minutes. Add the light soy sauce. Bring to a boil and turn off the heat. Let it stand overnight to give it thicker consistency and richer taste.

*Bikkuri-mizu (surprise water): Water added to beans while cooking. Add once or twice and the beans become soft and plump.

HIJIKI MIXED WITH VEGETABLES
Hijiki no gomoku-ni

INGREDIENTS

3/8 oz (10 g) dried hijiki (edible brown algae)
2 dried shiitake mushrooms
1 oz (30 g) carrot
1 3/4 oz (50 g) burdock
1 firm tofu (momen-dofu)
1 Tbsp vegetable oil

Simmering stock
1/2 cup dashi stock / 3 Tbsp sake / 2/3 Tbsp sugar /
2 Tbsp mirin / 2 1/2 Tbsp soy sauce / Dash salt

PREPARATION

■Hijiki
Break and wash briefly in water. Soak in ample water for 20 minutes. Scoop up gently in a bamboo colander, taking care not to scoop up the sand in the bottom. Drain. The soaked hijiki weighs 8 times heavier than the original dry hijiki.

■Vegetables, Tofu
Burdock: Make shaving cuts (sasagaki on p.12). Soak in vinegared water, then wash in water. Carrot: Cut into 1 1/4" (3 cm) long sticks (hyoshigi-giri on p. 11). Shiitake: Soak in water until soft. Discard stems and cut into thin slices. Tofu: Wrap in a thick dish-towel for 30 minutes.

METHOD — Japanese pan, 8 1/4" (21 cm)

1. Stir-fry vegetables and hijiki.

Heat the oil in a pan and stir-fry the burdock, carrot and shiitake over high heat. When the whole is coated well with oil, stir in the hijiki and fry together.

High heat

2. Add the tofu.

Crush the tofu roughly with hands. Mix in with a wooden spoon and stir-fry until coated well with the oil.

3. Add the simmering stock and lower the heat.

Add the dashi stock and seasoning and lower the heat to medium high. Continue cooking, stirring once in a while until the liquid is almost gone.

Medium high heat

4. Cook until the liquid is completely absorbed.

Slant the pan and cook until the liquid is completely absorbed. Transfer to a flat container and spread to cool. Serve in bowls.

*Other recipes for hijiki: Salads mixed with tofu dressing or vinegared miso dressing. When simmering, stir-fry in oil in advance for rich taste.

DRIED STRIPS OF DAIKON RADISH
Kiriboshi daikon no nimono

TIP
Don't add all the seasonings at once. Add the soy sauce later.

INGREDIENTS

1 oz (30 g) dried strips of daikon radish (kiriboshi daikon)
1 sheet aburage
Fresh daikon leaves

Simmering stock
1 1/2 cups dashi stock / 1 Tbsp sake / 1 1/2 Tbsp sugar /
1 Tbsp mirin / 2 Tbsp soy sauce / Dash salt

PREPARATION

■Dried strips of daikon radish
Rinse briefly under running water and soak in ample water for 15 minutes. Don't soak for a long time or the flavor and crispness are spoiled. Squeeze the water out gently. The soaked strips will become 5 times heavier than the dry ones.

■Aburage, Daikon leaves
Aburage: Pour boiling water over to remove the excess oil. Cut in half lengthwise and then into thin strips.
Daikon leaves: Parboil in salted water and cool in cold water. Drain and cut into thin strips.

METHOD
Japanese pan, 7" (18 cm)

1. Cook the dried daikon and then the aburage.

Bring the dashi stock to a boil in a pan. Add the daikon and bring to a boil again over medium heat. Add the aburage and bring to a boil again.

Medium heat

2. Add the sake and sugar.

Add the sake and sugar and cook for 2~3 minutes. Dried ingredients like kiriboshi daikon easily absorbs the seasonings, so add the soy sauce later or they will become salty.

3. Add the mirin, soy sauce and salt.

Add the mirin, soy sauce and salt. Continue cooking, stirring occasionally with chopsticks until the liquid is reduced and the ingredients around the edge of the pan dry up.

4. The liquid is completely reduced.

Slant the pan and cook until the remaining liquid is completely gone. Transfer to a flat container to cool. Serve in bowls with the daikon leaves scattered over.

***Kiriboshi daikon**: Fresh kiriboshi is white, but it turns to yellow as it gets old. Old kiriboshi should be soaked in water and then rinsed.

RECONSTITUTION of DRY GOODS

Dried Shiitake Mushrooms

Rinse briefly and soak in ample water for about half a day until tender. Place a small plate to prevent from floating. When in a hurry, soak in lukewarm water with a dash of sugar added.

Dried Wakame

Soak in ample water for about 5 minutes. Open and cut off the stem. Cut into bite-sized lengths. To bring out the color, place in a colander and pour boiling water over and then refresh in cold water.

Freeze-dried Tofu

Place in a flat container and soak in ample lukewarm water until tender. Put between hands and press from both sides under running water, gently squeezing out the water repeatedly until it is clear.

Kampyo (dried gourd strips)

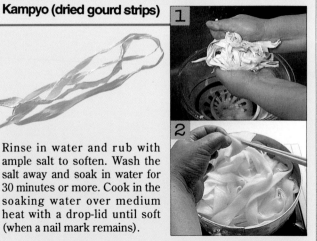

Rinse in water and rub with ample salt to soften. Wash the salt away and soak in water for 30 minutes or more. Cook in the soaking water over medium heat with a drop-lid until soft (when a nail mark remains).

Zenmai (royal fern)

Rinse briefly in water and then soak in ample water overnight. Boil for 7~8 minutes until soft. Cut off the hard part at the end and cut the whole into bite-sized pieces.

Harusame (starch noodles)

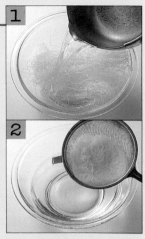

Place in a bowl and pour ample boiling water over. Soak in the water for 7~8 minutes until transparent. Drain and transfer to cold water. Drain and cut into bite-sized pieces.

TIPS FOR SIMMERED DISHES

Use the proper pan.

The first prerequisite is to select the proper pan which is suited to the quantity of ingredients.
If the ingredients are placed to fit the pan like the photo shown on the right, they will evenly be covered with the simmering stock and well seasoned. If the pan is too large, the stock will become insufficient, and if too small, the ingredients will stick out of the stock and they will not be seasoned evenly.

Sweet seasonings to be followed by salty ones.

First, bring the dashi stock to a boil and then add sake and sugar. Next, add mirin, soy sauce and salt in this order. Sugar takes time to be absorbed, so it is added first. Soy sauce and salt hardens ingredients, so they are added lastly.
If they are added vice versa, the food will become salty and lack in sweetness. Vegetables and meat are generally cooked in the dashi stock first and then seasonings are added.
Fish is cooked in the dashi stock which is seasoned previously.

Cook with a drop-lid.

The drop-lid is a lid, which is slightly smaller than the pan and drops directly onto the food. Simmering this way ensures that the food is well covered with the stock and evenly seasoned. The lid which fits the pan exactly is used only when boiling water. A wooden drop-lid is usually used, but aluminum foil is used for fish, which has strong smell and Japanese paper for taro, which easily breaks.
Be sure to soak the wooden drop-lid in water before use so that color and flavor may not cling to the lid.

Reducing the liquid.

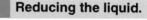

Dishes such as Braised Chicken and Braised Beef and Potatoes are cooked until the liquid is reduced, using a method called 'nabe-gaeshi' (turn over).
When the liquid is reduced to 1/3, turn over the ingredients by sliding them in the pan towards you. When you slant the pan, you will find the liquid still remains. Cook until the liquid has completely gone by slanting the pan.
A drop-lid is used when cooking juicy foods like koori-dofu (freeze-dried tofu). Cook until the pressed out liquid is evaporated.

After cooking handling is important.

Wrong handling of the cooked dishes spoils everything. The ingredients, which are cooked until the liquid is gone, should be spread on a flat container to cool. If they remain in the pan, they become soggy.
On the other hand, cooked beans should remain in the pan soaking in the liquid overnight.
Cooked fish should be served immediately while it is tasty.

BROILED AND PAN-FRIED DISHES

Yakimono

SALT-BROILED HORSE MACKEREL
Aji no shio-yaki

The best season to eat horse mackerel is summer. Carefully adjust the heat to broil the fish beautifully brown. Garnish the blue fish with grated daikon radish or grated ginger, which will get rid of the fishy odor.

INGREDIENTS

2 horse mackerel, each 7 oz (200 g)
2 Tbsp salt
Grated daikon radish
Grated ginger
2 slices lemon

TIPS

1. Broil the surface at some distance above high heat.
2. Serve immediately after broiled.

PREPARATION

1. Cleaning and dressing the fish.

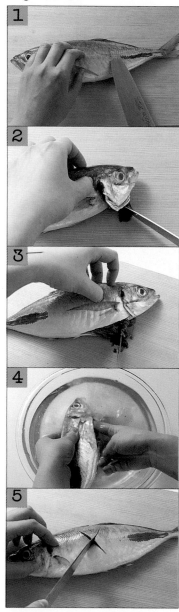

Remove the hard scales from the tail upward with a slanted knife.

Insert the knife under the gill opening and detach the base of the gill cover, drawing the red part out.

Place the head on the right. Make a slit between the gill and anal and draw the entrails out with a tip of the knife.

Insert a finger into the opening and remove remaining organs and blood and pat dry.

Place the head on the left and make crosswise slits on the body (*Yakimono-bocho).

2. Skewering.

Lay two fish with the heads on the left. First insert a metal skewer in the center, twisting and then right and left like a fan. The skewers cross at the end.

3. Salting.

Sprinkle salt over evenly from 12" (30 cm) above. So that the finish looks beautiful, dust salt over the tail, pectoral and dorsal fins (Kesho-jio). Cover the pectoral fin and tail with aluminum foil to prevent from burning.

Kesho-jio

*Yakimono-bocho: To make slits on the surface of the fish to heat through well and to prevent breaking off.

TO SERVE
Arrange the fish with the head on the left. Garnish with grated daikon radish and ginger on a slice of lemon.

METHOD   Grill and Iron Frame

1. Broil the serving side.

Place the grill on the iron frame. Broil the serving side at some distance above high heat. When about 60% cooked, turn them over.

Above high heat

2. Metal skewers come out easily when cooked.

If the skewers twist easily, the fish is done. While hot, pull them out, twisting.

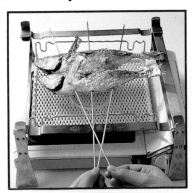

SALT-BROILED YELLOWTAIL

■Ingredients
4 fillets yellowtail, each 2 7/8 oz (80 g) / 1 Tbsp salt / Grated daikon radish / 2 slices lime

■Method
1. Lay the fillets on a cutting board, and thread 2 skewers like a fan.
2. Sprinkle salt over and broil the serving side at some distance above high heat.
3. When about 60% cooked, turn them over until skewers come out easily.
4. Garnish with grated daikon radish with a few drops of soy sauce added.

39

SPANISH MACKEREL SEASONED WITH YUAN-JIRU
Sawara no Yuan-yaki

TIP

Broil the seasoned fish at some distance above medium heat.

INGREDIENTS

2 fillets Spanish mackerel, each 3 1/2 oz (100 g)
2 sudori-shoga (vinegared ginger)

Yuan-jiru (stock)

Combine 1 Tbsp sake, 1 Tbsp mirin and 4 Tbsp soy sauce/
Prepare 1/2 citron slices

PREPARATION

■Spanish mackerel

Soak the fish in the stock and place the citron slices and turn over once in a while. Allow to stand for about 30 minutes until well seasoned.

■Sudori-shoga

Soak fresh ginger with leaves in boiling water. Dust with salt and soak in vinegar (see p. 152).

METHOD

Grill and Iron Frame

1. Thread skewers.

Arrange the fish in the same direction and thread 2 skewers crosswise in the center. Thin and long fillets should be skewered at right angles with the grain to prevent from breaking off.

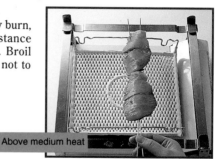

2. First broil the serving side.

Seasoned fillets easily burn, so broil at some distance above medium heat. Broil both sides with care not to burn.

Above medium heat

3. Baste with Yuan-jiru.

When about 90% cooked (the skewers twist easily), brush the fillets with the Yuan-jiru and place over the heat to dry. Repeat this twice on both sides.

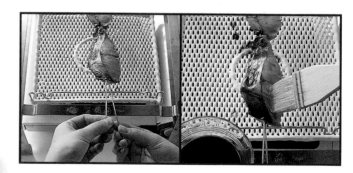

4. Pull out the skewers.

Pull out the skewers, twisting, while the fillets are hot. The meat will stick to the skewers if pulled out after cooled. Garnish with the sudori-shoga and serve.

BROILED CUTTLEFISH WITH EGG YOLK
Ika no kimi-yaki

Season the thick meat with salt and sake and dress with egg yolks.

TIPS
1. Score the inside to prevent from curling.
2. Brush with egg yolk several times and dry.

INGREDIENTS
1 cuttlefish, body (7 oz / 200 g)
{ 1/2 Tbsp sake
{ 1/2 tsp salt
Rape blossoms

Kimi-goromo
1 egg yolk / Dash salt

PREPARATION

■Cuttlefish

Buy an opened body (raw or frozen). Remove both sides and cut the body lengthwise into two in the center.

Lay inside up and score fine cross strips with a slanting knife.

Dress with salt and sake and allow to stand for about 5 minutes.

■Rape blossoms
Remove the hard parts near the root and boil in salted water.

METHOD
Grill and Iron Frame

1. Thread skewers.

Pat dry lightly. Lay horizontally on a cutting board and thread 3 metal skewers, twisting, in parallel.

2. Broil both sides.

First broil the scored side at some distance above high heat. When 60% cooked, turn over and broil the other side until the skewers twist easily.

Above high heat

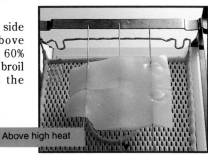

3. Brush the egg yolk.

Mix salt to the egg yolk and brush the scored side only. Pass over the heat quickly and dry. Repeat this 2 or 3 times. Pull out the skewers, twisting, while hot.

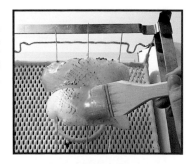

*Yuan-yaki: To soak fish in the liquid seasoned citron and broil. Tea master, Yuan is said to have created this method.

41

BROILED POMFRET IN SAIKYO-WAY

Managatsuo no saikyo-yaki

The white meat of the fish goes well with the saikyo-miso, lightly salted bean paste. The browned color is beautiful and the flavor of miso is exquisite.

TIPS

1. Wrap the fish in gauze to separate from miso.
2. Broil at some distance above medium heat to avoid burning.

INGREDIENTS

4 fillets pomfret, each 2 7/8 oz (80 g)
1/2 Tbsp salt
1/3 kiku-nori (dried chrysanthemum petals)

Ama-zu (sweet vinegar)

- 3 Tbsp dashi stock
- 1 1/2 Tbsp vinegar
- 1/2 Tbsp sugar
- Dash salt

Miso-doko

10 1/2 oz (300g) saikyo-miso / 3 Tbsp sake

PREPARATION

1. Season the fish.

Arrange the fillets on a bamboo colander and sprinkle salt over both sides. Let stand for about 30 minutes. When the surface is moistened, wipe carefully.

2. Make miso-doko

In a flat container, mix the saikyo-miso with sake. Set aside half the quantity.

3. Sandwich between miso layers.

Even out the miso in a flat container and cover with wet gauze, which is wrung out firmly. Lay the fillets on the gauze and cover with another gauze and then with remaining half of the miso.

4. Preserve for two nights.

METHOD Grill and Iron Frame

1. Thread skewers and broil the skin side.

Thread two fillets with two skewers, spreading out. Score slits crosswise on the skin. The fish seasoned with miso easily burn, so broil at some distance above medium heat. First broil the skin side. When 60% cooked, turn over.

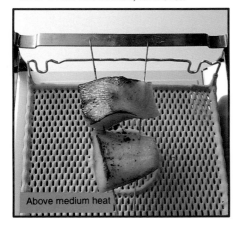

Above medium heat

2. Twist the skewers to check.

Broil the backside slowly. Twist the skewers and if they twist easily, the fish is done.

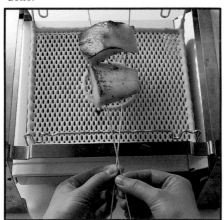

*The use of miso-doko:
Miso-doko can be stored in the refrigerator for about half a month. You can preserve salted foods in it, such as tilefish, chicken thigh and bluefish.

TO SERVE

It is ideal to warm the plate in hot water in advance when serving broiled foods. Parboil the kiku-nori as illustrated on page 115 and soak in ama-zu. If it is placed on a chrysanthemum leaf, early winter is suggested.

VARIATIONS OF BROILED FOODS

Kinome (for squid, clam, chicken breast, etc.)

20 pieces kinome
1 Tbsp sake
1 Tbsp light soy sauce

Combine sake and soy sauce. Add finely pounded kinome (young leaves of prickly ash). Marinate before broiling.

Arima (for beef, mackerel, Spanish mackerel, etc.)

1/2 tsp powdered Japanese pepper
1 Tbsp sake
1 Tbsp light soy sauce

Combine the ingredients. Marinate for about 5 minutes before broiling.

Uni (for whitefish, squid, etc.)

1 1/2 Tbsp neri-uni / 1/2 Tbsp sake

Neri-uni is paste of seasoned sea-urchin eggs. Dissolve neri-uni in sake and brush in the same way as shown on page 41.
Pass over heat briefly to dry.

Miso-zuke (for chicken thigh, cod, Spanish mackerel, etc.)

7 oz (200 g) miso
2 Tbsp sake
2 Tbsp mirin

Dissolve miso in sake and mirin. Marinate for about 1 hour before broiling.

BEEF TATAKI

Gyuniku no tataki

A simple and easy pan-fried dish. The sliced beef is seasoned with plenty of spices.

TIP

Pan-fry only the outside. Be careful not to overcook.

INGREDIENTS

10 1/2 oz (300 g) beef, boneless round
1/3 tsp salt
1/3 tsp pepper
1/2 Tbsp vegetable oil
Chives
1 slice small ginger root
1 clove garlic

1 Tbsp sake / 1 Tbsp soy sauce

PREPARATION

■Beef
Salt and pepper the beef just before pan-frying and rub in well.

■Spices
Cut the chives into thin round slices and grate the garlic and ginger.

METHOD

Frying pan

1. Pan-fry both sides.

Heat the frying pan and swirl the oil around. Add the beef. Fry the meat over medium heat until both sides are evenly browned. Turn the heat off.

Medium heat

2. Sprinkle the sake and soy sauce over.

Sprinkle the sake and soy sauce over the meat. Cover immediately as tightly as possible with a bowl and cook over low heat for about 7 minutes.

Low heat

3. Reduce the gravy and pour over.

Transfer the meat to a flat container and reduce the gravy in the frying pan to half. Pour the gravy over the meat and leave to cool. Store in the refrigerator and chill.

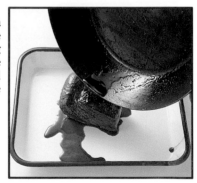

4. Slice the cooled meat.

Be sure to slice the meat after cooled. While hot it is hard to slice and the meat breaks. Cut the meat at a right angle with the grain.

*How to eat tataki: Eat with spices or together with sliced vegetables. You may also mix with dressing and sauce.

CHICKEN TERIYAKI

Toriniku no nabe-teriyaki

TIP

Pat the chicken with cornstarch before pan-frying.

INGREDIENTS

7 oz (200 g) chicken thighs
Cornstarch
1 Tbsp vegetable oil
10 aojiso (green shiso leaves)

2 Tbsp sake / 2 Tbsp sugar / 1 Tbsp mirin / 2 Tbsp soy sauce

PREPARATION

■Chicken thighs
Trim fat off the chicken and remove extra skin. Cut the chicken lengthwise in half and then diagonally into thin slices.

■Aojiso
Cut the leaves lengthwise in half and roll up. Cut into fine strips from the end. Rinse in water and squeeze it out.

*Nabe-teriyaki: Pan-fry ingredients, add the seasonings and cook until browned.

METHOD   Frying pan

1. Pat with cornstarch.

Prepare a gauze pack of cornstarch and pat the chicken evenly.

2. Remove the pan from the heat and arrange the meat.

Heat the frying pan and swirl the oil around. Remove the pan from the heat to prevent the meat added first from burning. Pat the chicken lightly with cornstarch, arrange the pieces on the pan.

3. Pan-fry both sides and discard the oil.

Pan-fry both sides of the chicken over medium heat until browned. Hold the pieces with chopsticks to cook well. Discard the extra oil.

Medium heat

4. Add the seasonings and cook.

Remove the pan from the heat again. Add the seasonings. Return to the heat. Cook over medium heat, shaking the pan and turning the chicken over 2~3 times until browned all over. Arrange on a plate with the strips of aojiso scattered over.

THICK OMELETS
Atsuyaki-tamago

One is a thick omelet of Edo-style, which is strongly seasoned with thick soy sauce and sugar, and another is a plain rolled omelet, which is seasoned with light soy sauce and dashi stock.

INGREDIENTS

■Rolled eggs with dashi	■Edo-style thick omelet
4 eggs	5 eggs
1/3 cup dashi stock	3 Tbsp sugar
1 tsp mirin	1 Tbsp mirin
1 tsp light soy sauce	2/3 Tbsp soy sauce
1/3 tsp salt	Dash salt
Vegetable oil	Vegetable oil

PREPARATION

Strain the egg mixture through a sieve.

① Break eggs in a bowl. Lift the whites up 3~4 times.
② Stir the eggs with chopsticks but do not beat.
③ Add the seasonings and mix well.
④ Strain through a sieve to make a smooth mixture.

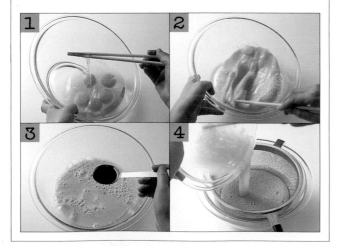

METHOD
Omelet pan

1. Coat a square omelet pan with oil.

Heat a square omelet pan and wipe the surface, four corners and sides, well with an oiled paper towel. Reduce the heat to medium until a drop of egg mixture sizzles.

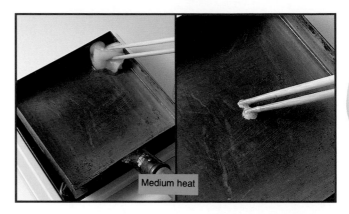

Medium heat

2. Pour in the egg mixture and cook until half done.

Pour in 1/3 of the egg mixture and spread evenly. Make even the swelled parts with chopsticks and cook until the surface is half done.

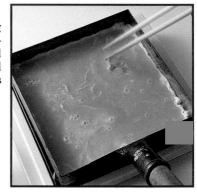

3. Fold into three layers.

Insert a chopstick between the edge of the pan and egg. Move the chopstick along the sides and free the egg from the pan. Fold the egg twice, starting from the further end, and into three layers.

*The back and front of a bamboo mat (makisu): Place an omelet or spinach on the corrugated side, and rolled sushi on the smooth side.

TO SERVE

Garnish with umezu-shoga (plum vinegared ginger), which has an acid taste, or green leaves like mitsuba (honewort).

4. Wipe the pan again with oil.

Oil the space and slide the folded egg toward the back of the pan. Wipe the rest of the pan with oil and pour in half of the remaining egg mixture. Lift the folded egg and let the mixture run under it. Cook until the surface is half done and fold in two toward you. Repeat this, making the roll bigger.

5. Shape with a bamboo mat.

Lay the cooked egg on the corrugated side of the bamboo mat. To shape, press the mat gently along its length with your fingers. Cut into slices.

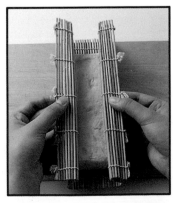

*Chigusa: Name given to the dish, which is a mixture of several kinds of ingredients.

OMELETS WITH FILLINGS

Broiled eel

■**Ingredients & Method:**

Season 4 eggs with 1/2 Tbsp each of sugar and mirin, 1 tsp light soy sauce and dash of salt. Cut a broiled eel into pieces and roll up with omelet.

Chigusa*

■**Ingredients & Method:**

Season 4 eggs with 1/2 Tbsp each of sugar and mirin, 1 tsp light soy sauce and dash of salt. Chop 3 chives, 2 slices of ham, a little carrot. Add all to the eggs and cook an omelet.

Pollack roe and mitsuba

■**Ingredients & Method:**

Stir 4 eggs. Add pollack roe sprinkled with 2 Tbsp sake and mitsuba (honewort) cut into big pieces. Cook an omelet.

TIPS FOR BROILED AND PAN-FRIED DISHES

◼ Pierce metal skewers through fish.

There are two methods of broiling fish: one is with metal skewers and the other over a gridiron. To make fish look pleasing to the eyes, skewer methods are recommended.

To skewer fish, place the meat near the edge of a cutting board. Pierce the skewers parallel to the board, twisting.

◆The whole fish
Place two fish near the edge of a cutting board with the heads facing left. Pierce 3 skewers above the middle bones so that they cross at the base and fan out the other ends.

◆Fillets
Pierce 2 skewers in the middle of the meat at the right angle with the grain to prevent the fish from breaking off while broiling.

◼ Salt and pepper just before broiling.

When broiling horse mackerel or beef tataki, sprinkle salt and pepper just before broiling. If sprinkled long before broiling, water oozes out of the fish and it burns easily. In the case of beef, savory gravy runs out of the meat.

◼ Broil the fish at some distance above the heat.

If broiled directly above the heat, the surface of the fish burns before the inside is cooked. It is, therefore, necessary to broil about 4" (10 cm) above the heat, using an iron frame. In case the iron frame is not available, use bricks. If a gridiron is placed above the heat, it will bring about an ideal effect as if cooked above charcoal. In the case of salted fish, broil over high heat, and seasoned fish should be cooked over medium heat.

◼ First broil the side to serve.

Start broiling from the side to serve. When broiling the whole fish, lay it with the head facing to right. In the case of fillets, first broil the skin side. When cooked 60%, turn over. Turn only once. If turned several times, the skin will peel and the meat will break off. When fish are cooked from the backside, the oily surface looks unpleasant when served.

◼ Twist the skewers to check.

If the skewers twist easily over the heat, the fish is done. Pull out the skewers while hot, twisting, and serve immediately.

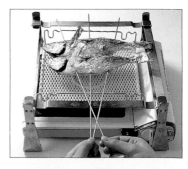

DEEP-FRIED DISHES

Agemono

TEMPURA

Strictly speaking, deep-fried fresh seafood is called 'tempura,' and deep-fried vegetables 'shojin-age.' However, both are served together at home.
Tempura goes well with 'tentsuyu' (tempura sauce) and shojin-age with soy sauce.

TO SERVE

Serve immediately after deep-frying. Spread absorbent paper on a plate and arrange the foods artistically. Serve with tempura sauce.

■ INGREDIENTS

1/4 small cuttlefish, 1 3/4 oz (50 g)
6 shrimp, each 2" (5~6 cm)
2 sillago (small white meat fish)
4 sweet pepper
1/2 eggplant, 1 3/4 oz (50 g)

1 1/2" (4 cm) burdock, 1 oz (30 g)
1 1/4" (3 cm) carrot, 1 oz (30 g)
1/4 lotus root, 1 3/4 oz (50 g)
1/5 sweet potato, 1 3/4 oz (50 g)

Batter
{ 1 small egg plus ice water to make 1 cup, lightly beaten
{ 1 cup flour
Flour, Toasted nori, Oil for deep-frying, Tentsuyu

TENTSUYU (Tempura sauce)

■Ingredients
1 cup water
1/4 cup mirin
1/4 cup light soy sauce
A handful of dried bonito flakes

■Method
1. Combine water and seasonings in a small pan. Add the bonito flakes and cook over high heat.
2. When it comes to a boil, turn off the heat and let stand to cool.
3. Strain through a damp cloth.

PREPARATION (Ingredients)

Remove harshness from the burdock and lotus root by soaking in vinegared water. Pat dry all the ingredients.

Cuttlefish
Wipe with a thoroughly wrung out wet cloth. Cut into pieces, 1 1/2" (4 cm) long and 3/4" (2 cm) wide. Make two scores crosswise.

Sweet pepper
Cut off the stems, leaving a bit near the end and make a cut lengthwise to prevent from bursting during cooking.

Eggplant
Cut off the stems and cut into round slices, 1/4" (5~6 mm) thick. Soak immediately in water for 3~4 minutes to remove harshness. Pat dry.

Shrimp
Remove the heads and devein. Place on a cutting board with belly side up and cut off the tips between tails to prevent oil from spattering during cooking.

Scrape off water from the tail with the tip of a knife.

Shell, leaving some near the tail. Make 2~3 cuts on the underside to prevent curling during cooking.

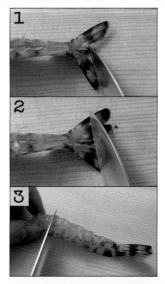

Sillago
Scrape off scales, cut off the head and remove entrails. Wash quickly in water. Pat dry and cut into 3 fillets. Remove bones (see page 154).

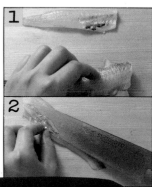

Burdock
Scrub with a brush under running water. Cut into fine strips, 2" (5~6 cm) long. Soak immediately in vinegared water to remove harshness. When the color of water changes, rinse and wipe dry.

Carrot
Peel and cut into fine strips, 2" (5~6 cm) long, the same length as the burdock.

Lotus root
Pare the thick skin and dip in vinegared water. Cut into round slices, 1/4" (5~6 mm) thick. Soak again in vinegared water for 3~4 minutes. Wash briefly in water and pat dry.

Sweet potatoes
Scrub with a brush under running water. Leaving the skin on, cut into round slices, 1/4" (5~6 mm) thick. Soak in water to remove harshness. Pat dry.

*Tempura: The word 'tempura' is said to come from Spanish 'tenpuro' (temple) or Portuguese 'tenpero' (cooking).

PREPARATION (Tempura batter)

Egg + ice water : Flour = 1 : 1
The quantity of beaten egg plus ice water is equal to that of flour.
Use pastry flour and ice water to make crisp tempura.

2. Mix the egg and ice water.
Break the egg in a large bowl and add ice water. Mix well.

4. Don't stir too much.
If stirred too much, the batter will become sticky and does not make crisp tempura. The batter should be thin and lumpy.

1. Sift the flour.
Sift the flour to add air. Air makes a light batter.

3. Add the flour.
Add the sifted flour all at once. Fold in lightly with chopsticks as if drawing crosses in the batter.

5. Add ice cubes.
Add one or two pieces of ice cubes to keep the batter chilled. Divide into 3 portions and store in the refrigerator to prevent from becoming sticky.

VARIATIONS OF BATTER

Shinbiki-ko
(rice powder, p.53)
Dredge with flour lightly, coat with egg white and dust with shinbiki-ko.

Harusame
(saifun noodles)
Dredge with flour lightly, coat with egg white and cover with harusame cut with scissors.

Aonori
(dried green laver)
Dredge with flour lightly and dip in batter mixed with aonori.

Yuba
(soy-milk skin, p.53)
Dredge with flour lightly, coat with egg white and cover with crumbled dried yuba.

Somen
(thin noodles)
Dredge with flour lightly, coat with egg white and cover with somen cut into small pieces.

*Kinpura and ginpura. Kinpura (golden) is a tempura deep-fried only with egg yellow and ginpura (silver) with egg white.

52

1. Sprinkle lightly with flour.

Sprinkle flour lightly over vegetables, except carrot and burdock, and seafood so that they are well coated with batter. If available, use chakoshi (tea strainer) to sprinkle with flour.

2. Start with vegetables.

The taste of deep-fried vegetables will not spoil even if they get cool, but seafood should be served immediately. Accordingly, start with vegetables.

Vegetables take time in deep-frying, so the oil temperature should be a little lower, 330~340°F(165~170℃).

330~340°F (165~170℃)

Tilt the batter in the bowl and coat the vegetables lightly using chopsticks. Don't turn in the batter repeatedly. Too much batter spoils the tempura, because the inside will be undercooked and the outside will be not crispy.

Carefully skim bits of fried batter off the oil. They make the tempura unsightly and the oil turbid. Remove them as often as possible.

To test for doneness, feel the fried batter with chopsticks. When the bubbles around the batter become smaller and the batter turns a crispy golden color, the tempura is done.

3. Deep-fried julienne vegetables.

Place the julienne vegetables in a bowl. Sprinkle with 1 tsp flour so as to be well coated with batter. Add 2 Tbsp batter, mix and coat. Pick up a bite-sized piece with chopsticks. Lay or slide in oil preheated 330~340°F (165~170℃) and deep-fry until crisp.

4. Deep-fried seafood.

Deep-fry fresh seafood at a higher oil temperature. Increase the temperature to 360 F°(180℃).

360°F (180℃)

Shrimp and sillago:
Hold the tail and dip into the batter and coat lightly. Slide into the oil from your side towards the other side. Skim the surface of the oil carefully and deep-fry slowly so as not to burn.

When aromatic and it feels crispy to the touch of chopsticks, it is done. Transfer to a flat container and drain well.

Cuttlefish:
Wrap in a toasted nori seaweed strip and paste the ends with batter. Coat lightly with batter and deep-fry until crisp.

* ninbiki-ko: Glutinous rice steamed, dried, and made into flour.

*Yuba: Dried skin that is formed when soy milk is cooked.

MIXED TEMPURA OF KOBASHIRA AND MITSUBA

Kobashira to mitsuba no kakiage

TIP

Divide into small portions and deep-fry one at a time.

INGREDIENTS

5 1/4 oz (150 g) kobashira (adductor of a round clam)
2 small bunches mitsuba (honewort) /2 tsp flour
Oil for deep-frying
Batter
3/4 cup mixture of 1 beaten egg and ice water / 3/4 cups flour
Tentsuyu (tempura sauce)

PREPARATION

■Kobashira
Rinse in a colander under the running water while shaking and pat dry.

■Mitsuba
Wash briefly in water and drain. Cut into pieces, 3/4" (2 cm) long.

■Tentsuyu
See page 50.

■Batter
Prepare as shown on page 52.
The batter should be lumpy.

METHOD

Deep-fry pan

1. Combine the ingredients and batter in a small bowl.

Divide the kobashira and mitsuba into two portions. Sprinkle 1 tsp flour over and mix lightly. Add 2 Tbsp batter and mix well.

2. Slide into the hot oil.

Scoop with a ladle and slide gently into the hot oil (350°F / 175°C) along the edge of the pan, taking care not to break up. Continue to hold with chopsticks until shape is well formed.

350°F (175°C)

3. Prick the surface with chopsticks.

When the edges began to get hard, turn it over. Cook for a while and then turn it over again. Prick the center with chopsticks 2 or 3 times to let the oil pass so that the inside is cooked well.

4. Cook until the inside gets crisp.

When the whole is deep-fried until crisp, transfer to a flat container and drain. Arrange on a plate and serve with tentsuyu.

DEEP-FRIED MARINATED PORK
Butaniku no tatsuta-age

TIPS
1. Soak pork in ginger-flavored marinade.
2. Use cornstarch to deep-fry to a crisp.

INGREDIENTS

7 oz (200 g) sliced pork
Marinade
  1 Tbsp sake
  1 1/2 Tbsp soy sauce
  2 tsp ginger juice
Cornstarch
1/2 pack kaiwarena (daikon radish sprouts)
2 cherry tomatoes
Oil for deep-frying

VARIATIONS OF MIXED TEMPURA

Shrimp and Mitsuba

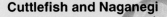

Devein, shell and remove head and tail of 16 shrimps. Cut 2 bunches of mitsuba into 3/4" (2 cm) lengths. Deep-fry in the same way as on page 54.

Cuttlefish and Naganegi

Cut 7 oz (200 g) cuttlefish into 3/8" (1 cm) cubes. Cut 2/3 naganegi into thin round slices. Deep-fry until crisp in the same way as on page 54.

Chikuwa and Onion

Cut chikuwa (broiled fish-paste cake) into 1/4" (5 mm) thick. Cut onion into 3/8"(1 cm) cubes. Deep-fry until crisp as on page 54.

PREPARATION

■Pork slices
Cut into bite-sized pieces. Soak in marinade mixture and let stand for about 5 minutes.

■Kaiwarena
Cut into 1 1/4"(3 cm) lengths.

METHOD

Preheat oil to 350°F (175°C). Drain the pork and dust with cornstarch lightly. Slide into the oil.

Deep-fry until golden brown. Test for crispness with chopsticks. Drain well and serve on plates. Scatter the kaiwarena over and garnish with cherry tomatoes.

350°F (175°C)

*Tatsuta-age: The name comes from the Tatsuta river in Nara prefecture, which is famous for its tinted autumnal leaves. The color of tempura looks like maple leaves.

DEEP-FRIED PUFFY TOFU

Agedashi-dofu

The tofu is served with plenty of condiments and a delicious sauce. It is a very satisfying dish.

TIPS

1. Do not drain the tofu completely or the taste will be spoiled.
2. Deep-fry at high temperature until crisp and serve immediately.

INGREDIENTS

1 block kinugoshi-dofu (silken tofu)
Cornstarch
3 stalks scallions
Bonito flakes
Grated daikon radish
Chili peppers (momiji-oroshi) (store-bought)
White sesame seeds

Sauce

1/2 cup dashi stock / 1 Tbsp sake / 1 Tbsp light soy sauce /
1 tsp mirin

PREPARATION

■Kinugoshi-dofu

Wrap the tofu in a thick kitchen cloth and place in a flat container. Refrigerate for about 20 minutes and drain lightly. Cut into 8 portions.

■Condiments

Cut scallions into thin round slices. Grate the daikon radish and remove excess water. Toast sesame seeds with care not to burn.

■Sauce

Bring the dashi stock to a boil in a small pan and add other ingredients one by one.

METHOD

Deep-fry pan

1. Dust the tofu lightly with cornstarch.

Preheat the oil to 360°F (180°C). Dust the tofu lightly with cornstarch. Gently slide into the oil and deep-fry.

360°F (180°C)

2. Deep-fry until crisp.

Deep-fry until the tofu starts to change color and become crisp. When it comes to the surface, it is done. Remove and drain on a wire rack.

TO SERVE

Arrange the piping hot tofu in dishes and top with the condiments. Pour the sauce around the sides.

*Flour variation: You may use flour instead of cornstarch. The cornstarch makes the finish light and flour crunchy.

DEEP-FRIED POND SMELTS IN NANBAN-ZU
Wakasagi no nanban-zuke

TIPS

1. Soak smelts in milk to remove the fishy smell.
2. Pat the smelts dry to prevent the oil from spattering.
3. Marinate hot smelts in nanban-zu to season.

INGREDIENTS

12 pond smelts
⎡ 3/4 cup milk
⎢ 1/3 tsp salt
⎨ Dash pepper
⎣ Dash flour
2/3 naganegi (Japanese bunching onion)
1/2 stalk celery
Carrot
Oil for deep-frying

Nanban-zu
1/3 cup dashi stock / 1/2 cup vinegar / 1/2 tsp salt / Dash pepper
/ 1 Tbsp light soy sauce / 1 chili pepper

TO SERVE

Arrange the fish with the heads on the left and pour the nanban-zu over.

PREPARATION

■Pond smelts
Soak in milk for 30 minutes. Drain in a colander and pat dry with paper towel. Sprinkle with salt and pepper.

■Vegetables
Remove veins of the celery and the core of the naganegi. Cut the celery, naganegi and carrot into 1 1/2" (4 cm) lengths. Remove seeds from the chili pepper and cut into fine pieces.

■Nanban-zu
Combine the ingredients of nanban-zu in a tilted flat container raised on one side and add the chili pepper.

METHOD   Deep-fry pan

1. Dust smelts lightly with flour.

Pat the sides of the smelts with a pack of flour in gauze. Preheat the oil to 350°F (175°C).
Slide into the hot oil.

350°F (175°C)

2. Soak immediately in nanban-zu.

Deep-fry until golden brown and crisp.
Immediately soak in the nanban-zu while still sizzling. When cooled, fried things do not season well.

3. Cover with vegetables and let stand for 1 hour.

Scatter the vegetables over the smelts and let stand for 1 hour until flavored with vegetables and nanban-zu.

*Nanban: The name is given to dishes which use chili pepper and naganegi. Also it is used for sautéed and deep-fried dishes.

TIPS FOR DEEP-FRIED DISHES

Pan

It is important to use a deep, wide and heat-retaining pan to make crisp tempura.

The best tempura pan is the one which is made of copper, but a wok which has a round bottom is also good.

Never use a shallow pan, because the oil overflows when ingredients are added and there is a danger of fire.

Deep-fry pan   Wok

Oil

Use either vegetable oil or tempura oil as desired. The quality of the oil deteriorates as it is used, and deep-fried foods lose crispness and become brown. Use new oil when deep-frying seafood, vegetables and tofu, to avoid discoloration. When the oil deteriorates, add new oil. When frying marinated or seasoned ingredients, used oil will be appropriate, since they are well browned. After deep-frying, remove bits of fried batter from the surface of the oil and drain. Store in a cool place, taking care not to expose to the air to prevent oxidizing.

Temperatures

Crisp tempura depends on the temperature of oil. It must be not too high or too low. A thermometer is necessary to measure the exact temperature, but when not available, you can test it by the methods shown on the right.

The quantity of ingredients should be kept less than half of the surface area of oil. If you add too much at once, the temperature drops lower.

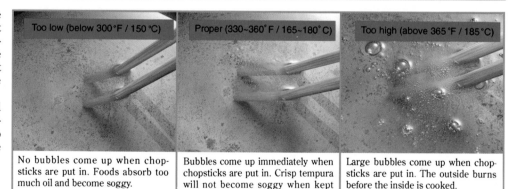

Too low (below 300°F / 150°C)	Proper (330~360°F / 165~180°C)	Too high (above 365°F / 185°C)
No bubbles come up when chopsticks are put in. Foods absorb too much oil and become soggy.	Bubbles come up immediately when chopsticks are put in. Crisp tempura will not become soggy when kept long.	Large bubbles come up when chopsticks are put in. The outside burns before the inside is cooked.

Various Ways to Eat Tempura

Tentsuyu is not the only sauce, which is good for tempura. Try to eat with citrus fruits like lemon, the mixture of powdered tea and salt or the mixture of pepper and salt.

Lemon   Powdered tea & salt   Japanese pepper & salt

Paper

When arranging tempura on an unglazed container or a piece of lacquer ware, spread paper under it. Place the paper with the folded side towards you and shift the corners a little.

STEAMED DISHES

Mushimono

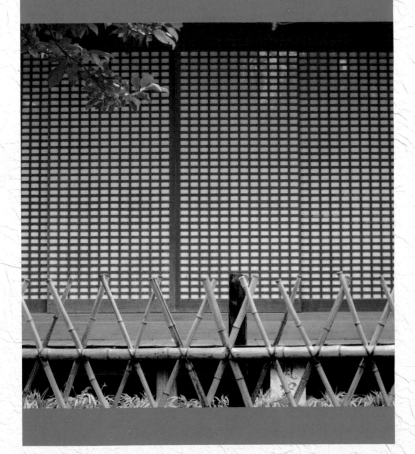

STEAMED EGG CUSTARD

Chawan-mushi

This savory custard features tasty morsels of chicken and mushrooms and colorful ginkgo nuts, ume-bu and mitsuba. Relish the soft and smooth texture.

(**Ume-bu**: Wheat gluten colored and shaped like an ume plum blossom)

TIPS

1. Don't beat eggs and add plenty of dashi stock. Strain.
2. Divide ingredients and egg mixture into two and cook each.
3. Steam slowly over low heat.

INGREDIENTS

3 1/2 oz (100 g) skinless
   chicken breasts
2 fresh shiitake mushrooms
1/2 tsp light soy sauce
6 shelled ginkgo nuts
2 slices each of red and white
   kamaboko
1 1/4" (3 cm) ume-bu
Mitsuba (honewort)

Custard base
{
2 eggs
1 1/2 cups dashi stock
1 tsp sake
2/3 tsp salt
1 tsp light soy sauce
}

TO SERVE

As the container is also hot, serve it on a saucer. If lacquer ware is used as the saucer, place paper on it to avoid damage (paper, p.58).

PREPARATION

1. Ingredients

■ **Chicken breasts, Shiitake mushrooms**
Remove the skin and tendons from the chicken and cut into thin slices. Wipe dirt from mushroom caps with a wet dishtowel. Cut off the stems and coarsely chop. Sprinkle 1/2 tsp light soy sauce over the chicken and mushrooms.

■ **Ginkgo nuts, Ume-bu, Mitsuba**
Shell the ginkgo nuts. Parboil in salted water and peel the skin (see page 115). Cut the ume-bu into 1/4" (5 mm) thick slices and blanch in boiling water. Cut the mitsuba (honewort) into 2" (5 cm) long pieces.

2. Custard base

Ratio of eggs to dashi stock is 1 to 3.

① Break eggs into a large bowl. Use the cooking chopsticks to lift up the egg whites 3 or 4 times. Stir with the chopsticks, but do not beat.
② Stirring with the chopsticks, gradually add the dashi stock. Add the remaining ingredients for the custard and mix well.
③ Strain through a sieve to make smooth texture.

*Ingredients good for the steamed egg custard: Whitefish, kinugoshi-dofu and mushrooms.

60

1. First steam the ingredients hard to cook.

Some ingredients are cooked easily and others are not. Cook them separately. Place the chicken and shiitake evenly in each container. Fill with the custard to four-fifths full.

2. High and then low heat.

Transfer the containers to preheated steamer and cover with a lid wrapped in a dishtowel. Cook over high heat for 1 minute, reduce the heat and cook over low heat for about 15 minutes.

High heat → Low heat

Lowering the heat

Lower the heat and insert a bamboo skewer under the lid to release the steam properly.

3. Test for doneness with a bamboo skewer.

To test for doneness, insert a skewer into the center of the custard. If clear liquid comes out, it is done. Add the kamaboko, ginkgo nuts and ume-bu to each container. Pour 2 Tbsp custard base over. When bubbles come out on the surface, move to the edge of the container and crush.

4. Steam for another 3~4 minutes.

Cover again with the lid and steam for another 3~4 minutes. Finish up by garnishing with the mitsuba.

CUSTARD IN A BOWL

When steaming the custard, the lid of the container is unnecessary, so it is possible to use a teacup or a small bowl. You may also use a large bowl to steam all at once for a party or a get-together. The method and heating are the same, but steam for a little longer time, about 18 minutes.

STEAMED TILEFISH AND TURNIP
Amadai no kabura-mushi

Originally a large turnip is used, but any turnip will do.

INGREDIENTS

1 fillet tilefish, 3 1/2 oz (100 g)	**(A)**
2 shrimp	⎰ 1/4 egg white
2 fresh shiitake mushrooms	⎱ 2/3 tsp sake
Carrot	⎱ Dash salt
1/2 lily bulb	
6 ginkgo nuts	
1/2 bunch mitsuba (honewort)	**Kuzu-an**

Simmering stock
⎰ 1/2 cup dashi stock
⎱ 1/2 Tbsp sake
⎱ 2 Tbsp mirin
⎱ 1 Tbsp light soy sauce
10 1/2 oz (300 g) turnip

Kuzu-an
⎰ 3/4 cup dashi stock
⎱ 2/3 tsp sake
⎱ 1/3 tsp salt
⎱ Dash light soy sauce
⎱ 1 tsp cornstarch

Wasabi (Japanese horseradish)

TIPS

1. Steam over high heat for a short time.
2. Bring the kuzu-an to a boil to remove the smell of cornstarch.

PREPARATION

■Ingredients

Cut the tilefish in half. Devein the shrimp, parboil in salted water, shell and remove the head and cut in half. Wipe the cap of shiitake with a wet dishtowel, remove the stem and cut into thin slices. Cut the carrot in julienne strips. Remove fibrous roots from the lily bulb and rinse. Separate the stems, parboil in a little vinegared water until soft and let cool in a bamboo colander (see p. 115).

■Ginkgo nuts, Mitsuba
Prepare ginkgo nuts as shown on p.115. Cut the mitsuba into 2" (5 cm) lengths.

■Turnip
Peel the turnip, grate and wring lightly. Combine with (A).

METHOD
Steamer

1. Cook all the ingredients except shrimp.

Boil the simmering stock in a small pan and add the tilefish. When it comes to a boil, add vegetables, cover with a drop-lid of aluminum foil and cook over medium heat for 3~4 minutes. Divide the cooked ingredients, shrimp and ginkgo nuts into two bowls. Cover with half of the grated turnip.

2. Steam over high heat and cover with kuzu-an.

Spread a dishtowel on a preheated steamer. Place the bowl on top and steam over high heat for 5~6 minutes. In the meantime, combine the ingredients of kuzu-an. Cook over medium heat, stirring until thickened. Pour the kuzu-an over the steamed ingredients, top with wasabi and garnish with the mitsuba.

*Fish good for steaming with turnip: Whitefish with thick meat, such as flounder and plaice.

CHIRI-MUSHI OF BLUEFISH

Mutsu no chiri-mushi

The steamed whitefish with tofu is called 'chiri-mushi.' The chives and grated daikon bring out the delicate taste. Eat with pon-zu shoyu.

TIP

Steam over high heat in a preheated steamer.

INGREDIENTS

2 fillets mutsu (Japanese bluefish), each 3 1/2 oz (100 g)
1/3 tsp salt / 1 Tbsp sake
2 sheets kombu kelp, each 6 × 2"(15 × 5 cm)
1/3 block kinugoshi-dofu (silken tofu)
1/2 bunch chives
Daikon radish
1 small red hot pepper
Pon-zu shoyu (p. 157)

PREPARATION

■Bluefish
Sprinkle with sake and salt and allow to stand for about 10 minutes.

■Kombu, Tofu, Chives
Wipe the kombu with a dry dishtowel and remove dirt. Cut the tofu into 4 portions. Cut the chives into fine slices.

■Daikon
Insert seeded hot pepper into the daikon and grate (p. 152).

METHOD

Steamer

1. Place the fish and tofu on the kombu.

Spread the kombu in a bowl. Place the fish with the skin side up and the tofu in front.

2. Steam over high heat.

Spread a dishtowel in a preheated steamer. Insert the bowl and steam over high heat for 12~13 minutes.

High heat

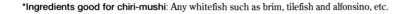

TO SERVE

Put the chives and grated daikon on the hot fish. Pour the pon-zu shoyu over as desired.

*Ingredients good for chiri-mushi: Any whitefish such as brim, tilefish and alfonsino, etc.

TIPS FOR STEAMED DISHES

Use plenty of boiled water.

It is very important to preheat the steamer well before cooking. If started with cold water, the foods will break up and the fish will have fishy odor. Prepare plenty of boiled water to avoid being forced to add in the middle of cooking.

In the case of a double steamer, fill the boiling water up to 70% of the under steamer. If a steaming plate is available, fill up to just below the plate.

Rice must be steamed for a long time, and if it becomes necessary to add water midway, add boiling water, not cold water.

Place a dishtowel in the steamer.

Take care when removing the cooked dishes from the hot steamer. By placing a folded dry dishtowel under the container as shown in the photo, you can remove the container by holding both ends of the dishtowel. However, this method can not be used when several cups are steamed together.

Insert a dishtowel under the lid.

When steaming, drops of water fall from the back of the lid. To avoid this, place a dry dishtowel under the lid. The dripping water makes holes in the food or makes the food watery. Be sure to fold the ends of the dishtowel up on the lid to avoid burning.

Except for egg dishes steam over high heat.

In principle, all the dishes are steamed over high heat except those using eggs. Fish and meat steamed over low heat have fishy odor and rice becomes sticky.

On the contrary, if egg dishes are steamed over high heat, the custard will have lots of pores and lose its taste. To check the doneness of the egg custard, insert a bamboo skewer. If clear liquid comes out, it is finished.

Tools for steaming

Japanese people usually use metal steamers, but Chinese bamboo steamers are also useful. The lid is made of woven bamboo and steam escapes through it. No drops of water fall, so a dishtowel is unnecessary.

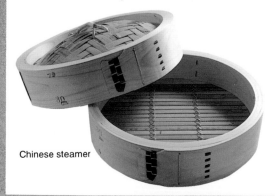

Chinese steamer

●When steamers are unavailable:

It is possible to steam foods without steamers. Place a small plate in a deep pot and cover with boiled water. Put the container on the plate and use the pot as a steamer. It is difficult to apply this method for the chawanmushi (steamed egg custard), but it is good for 'chiri-mushi.'

VINEGARED AND DRESSED DISHES

Aemono/Sunomono

CHRYSANTHEMUM TURNIP IN SWEETENED VINEGAR
Kikka-kabu no amazu-zuke

Cut the turnip as thin as possible, but not all the way through, like a flower of white chrysanthemum. Soak in ama-zu (sweetened vinegar).
Served as one of the festive foods for the New Year and as an hors d'oeuvre. It also can be used as a chopstick rest.

TIPS

1. Use chopsticks to make even slices.
2. Soak in salted water to soften.

INGREDIENTS

6 small turnips, each 1 3/4 oz (50 g)
1 red hot pepper

Ama-zu (sweetened vinegar)
1/2 cup vinegar / 2 Tbsp sugar / Dash salt / 1/3 cup dashi stock

TO SERVE

Squeeze out the ama-zu lightly before placing in the container. Use a bamboo skewer to place a slice of hot pepper in the middle.

PREPARATION

■Turnip
① Cut off the stem and leaves. Cut horizontally into rounds and peel off the skin.
② Place the stem side down. Lay chopsticks in front and back. They prevent the knife from cutting all the way through. Score the round crisscross.
③ Soak in salted water (1 Tbsp salt to 2 cups water) for about 20 minutes to make them pliable. Squeeze out the water.

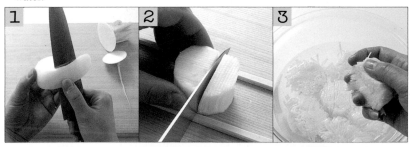

■Red hot pepper
Soak in water to make it tender. Cut off the calyx. Remove the seeds with a bamboo skewer. Cut into thin round slices.

METHOD

1. Make ama-zu.

Place the sugar and salt in a bowl and dissolve in vinegar. Add the dashi stock and red pepper slices.

2. Soak for half a day.

Soak turnips in the ama-zu and allow to stand for half a day until well seasoned.

*Ingredients good for ama-zu: Any vegetables. Not good for seafoods.

ARK SHELLS AND RAPE BLOSSOMS WITH NIHAI-ZU

Akagai to nanohana no nihai-zu

INGREDIENTS

3 ark shells, shelled
1/4 bunch rape blossoms

Nihai-zu
1 Tbsp vinegar / 1 Tbsp light soy sauce / 2 Tbsp dashi stock

PREPARATION

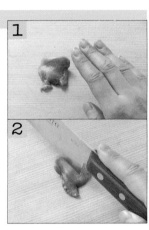

Buy shelled ark shells with ligaments and entrails removed. Coat with plenty of salt and rub with force. Rinse under running water and pat dry. Pound against a cutting board. Make fine scores on the thick part of the meat.

Cut off stems of rape blossoms, 3/4" (2 cm) from roots. Parboil in salted water. Transfer to cold water and wring out the water. Cut into bite-sized pieces.

METHOD

Combine the ingredients of the nihai-zu and mix well. Chill in a refrigerator until serving time.

TO SERVE
Arrange the ark shells and rape blossoms in a container. Pour the nihai-zu over from side.

CUCUMBER AND WAKAME WITH SANBAI-ZU

Kyuri to wakame no sanbai-zu

INGREDIENTS

3 1/2 oz (100 g) cucumber
3/16 oz (5 g) dry wakame
2 myoga (Japanese ginger)

Sanbai-zu
1 1/2 Tbsp vinegar / 1/2 Tbsp sugar / 1 Tbsp light soy sauce /
1 1/2 Tbsp dashi stock

PREPARATION

Cucumber: Sprinkle salt and roll on a board. Rinse in water and cut into thin slices. Soak in salted water until soft. Wring out water.

Wakame: Soak in water for 5 minutes. Remove strings and cut into 3/4" (2 cm) lengths. Soak in boiled water and then in cold water.

Myoga: Cut into thin pieces.

Place in a strainer and dip in boiling water and then in cold water. Drain.

METHOD

Combine the ingredients of the sanbai-zu and mix well. Chill in refrigerator together with other ingredients until the serving time.

TO SERVE
Arrange the ingredients in a container with balance in mind. Pour the sanbai-zu over from side.

*Ingredients good for the nihai-zu: Seafood such as octopus and squid.
*Ingredients good for the sanbai-zu: Udo plant, honewort, Chinese yam and chrysanthemum blossoms.

67

CUTTLEFISH AND CUCUMBER WITH KIMI-ZU
Ika to kyuri no kimi-zu

TIP

When making kimi-zu (golden yolk sauce), keep stirring until smooth.

INGREDIENTS

1/2 cuttlefish, 3 1/2 oz (100 g)
Dash vinegar
3 1/2 oz (100 g) cucumber

Kimi-zu
2 eggs yolk / 2 Tbsp mirin / 1 1/2 Tbsp vinegar / Dash salt

PREPARATION

■Cuttlefish
① Cut in half lengthwise and then cut each in half crosswise. Cut into julienne strips.
② Place in a bamboo colander and pour hot water over. Fan to cool and sprinkle with vinegar.

■Cucumber
Sprinkle with salt and roll on a cutting board. Wash the salt away.

Make thin slices diagonally as deep as 2/3. Turn over and do the same on the other side.

Soak in salted water until soft. Tear into bite-sized pieces. Squeeze the water out.

Jabara-giri (snake cuts)

TO SERVE
Heap the cuttlefish and cucumber in individual plates and top with kimi-zu.

METHOD

1. Combine ingredients for kimi-zu.

Combine the yolk and mirin in a small pan and stir with a wooden ladle. Add the salt and vinegar and mix well.

2. Heat in hot water to thicken.

Place the pan in a larger pan with hot water and cook over medium heat. Keep stirring with a wooden spatula until thickened. Cool and let stand until chilled.

Medium heat

*Ingredients good for kimi-zu: Shrimp, squid and lily bulbs.

68

UDO AND BROAD BEANS IN UME DRESSING

Udo to soramame no ume-ae

INGREDIENTS

9 oz (250 g) udo
10 1/2 oz (300 g) broad beans (with pods)
Kimi-soboro (strained boiled egg yolk)

Ume dressing
1 umeboshi (pickled plum) / 1 tsp mirin

PREPARATION

■Udo
Cut in half and peel the thick skin. Soak in water with 1~2 drops of vinegar added.
Cut, rolling, into pieces (ran-giri) and soak again in vinegared water. Rinse in water and drain.

■Broad beans
Shell and make small cuts (1/8" / 3 mm deep) at the bottom of each bean so it will peel easily. Boil in water with a dash of salt added for about 2 minutes. Transfer to a bamboo colander to cool. Remove the skins.

METHOD

Remove the stone from the pickled plum. Chop the flesh into fine pieces. Place in a bowl and add the mirin gradually. Combine the broad beans and udo and coat with the ume mixture. Place in individual bowls and top with the kimi-soboro.

*Ingredients good for the ume dressing: Chinese yam, squid and whitefish.

OCTOPUS AND BUTTERBUR WITH KARASHI-ZU

Tako to fuki no karashi-zu

INGREDIENTS

1 octopus leg, 7 oz (200 g)
8 butterbur, each 8" (20 cm) long

Karashi-zu
1 tsp dissolved mustard (Japanese mustard made from powder) / 1 1/2 Tbsp vinegar / 1 Tbsp light soy sauce / 1 Tbsp dashi stock

PREPARATION

■Butterbur
Sprinkle salt over and roll on a cutting board. Boil and transfer to cold water. Peel and cut into 2" (5 cm) lengths (see page 18).

■Octopus leg
Wash in water and pat dry. Cut off the tip (which sometimes contains sand). Cut diagonally into thin slices.

METHOD

Karashi-zu: place the mustard in a bowl. Add seasonings and dashi stock gradually. Place the octopus and butterbur in individual bowls and fill with karashi-zu.

*Ingredients good for the karashi-zu: Komatsuna, bracken and rape blossoms.

ROUND CLAMS AND SCALLIONS WITH KARASHI SU-MISO

Aoyagi to wakegi no nuta

TIP

Add mustard and vinegar to neri-miso (sweetened miso) to make karashi su-miso.

INGREDIENTS

1 3/4 oz (50 g) round clams (shelled)
1 tsp vinegar
4 scallions

Karashi su-miso

Neri-miso < 1/2 cup saikyo-miso / 2 Tbsp sugar / 1/2 cup mirin >
+2 tsp dissolved mustard / 1 Tbsp vinegar

*To make it easier, divide the neri-miso into three parts, adding the mustard and vinegar to each.

PREPARATION

■Scallions

① Put the white end into boiling water into which dash salt has been added. Guide green parts down into water and around the pan. Transfer to a bamboo colander and fan to cool.
② Lay on a cutting board. Squeeze out any stickiness from the green parts by pressing with a knife toward the ends. Cut into bite-sized lengths.

■Round clams

① Place in a bamboo colander. Rinse, shaking under running water. Parboil. Transfer to cold water immediately and drain.
② Sprinkle with vinegar and season lightly.

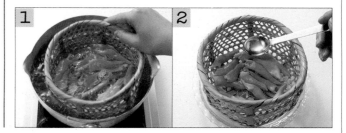

METHOD

1. Add sugar and mirin to miso.

Divide the miso into three parts, and make the neri-miso one at a time. Combine the miso and sugar in a small pan and mix with a wooden spoon. Add the mirin a little at a time, several times, and mix well until smooth.

2. Thicken over heat.

Cook over medium heat, stirring continuously. Turn off the heat when thickened.

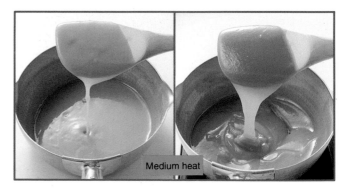

Medium heat

*Ingredients good for karashi su-miso: Octopus, udo, barilla and vinegared mackerel.

BAMBOO SHOOT AND CUTTLEFISH WITH KINOME-MISO
Takenoko to ika no kinome-miso

The taste of spring. You may make use of the neri-miso on previous page to make the kinome-miso.

INGREDIENTS

1 3/4 oz (50g) boiled bamboo shoot
1/4 cuttlefish, 1 3/4 oz (50g)
1/3 udo
Kinome (young leaves of prickly ash)

Simmering stock
- 2 Tbsp dashi stock
- 1 Tbsp mirin
- 1/2 Tbsp light soy sauce

Kinome-miso
3 Tbsp saikyo-miso / 1/2 Tbsp sugar / 1 Tbsp vinegar / 15 leaves kinome

PREPARATION

① Peel the thick skin of the udo. Cut the udo, bamboo shoots and cuttlefish into 1/2" (1.5 cm) cubes. Plunge the udo into vinegared water to remove the harshness and rinse and drain.
② Bring the simmering stock to a boil in a small pan and cook the bamboo shoots for 2~3 minutes.
③ Add the cuttlefish and cook briefly. Add the udo and turn the whole over and cook briefly.
④ Transfer to a bamboo colander and drain. Chill in the refrigerator.

METHOD

Combine the saikyo-miso and sugar in a bowl and mix well with a wooden spatula. Add the vinegar at two intervals. Add chopped kinome to make the kinome-miso. Dress the prepared ingredients.

3. Add mustard and vinegar to neri-miso.

Combine 3 Tbsp neri-miso, prepared mustard and vinegar in a bowl. Add round clams and scallions and heap in containers to serve.

Freeze neri-miso and store in freezer

It is possible to freeze and store the neri-miso, so make a little more than needed. When mixed up, let it cool completely and then transfer to an airtight container to store in the freezer. Thaw in the refrigerator before using.

*Ingredients good for kinome-miso: Tara-no-me (buds of aralia), tofu and konnyaku (devil's tongue jelly).

HORSE MACKEREL AND NEGI WITH SU-MISO
Aji to naganegi no su-miso

Su-miso is simple and easy to make. Just combine the miso with seasonings. If soaked in salted vinegar, the horse mackerel will improve in taste.

INGREDIENTS

1 horse mackerel, 7 oz (200 g)
1 naganegi (Japanese bunching onion)

Su-miso
3 Tbsp miso / 1 Tbsp sugar / 1 1/2 Tbsp vinegar

PREPARATION

Horse mackerel: Cut into three pieces and remove bones (see page 154). Coat the skin with vinegar to make it easy to peel. Skin from the head towards the tail. Cut into slices.
Naganegi: Parboil in water with a dash of salt added retaining firmness. Cool in a bamboo colander. Cut into 1 1/4" (3 cm) lengths and sprinkle with a few drops of vinegar.

METHOD

Combine the miso and sugar in an earthenware mortar. Add the vinegar and mix until smooth. Chill dressing and ingredients and mix well just before serving.

TOFU DRESSING
Shira-ae

TIPS
1. Pass the tofu through a fine sieve.
2. Chill the ingredients completely before mixing.

INGREDIENTS

1 1/2 oz (40 g) carrot
3 dried shiitake mushrooms
1/2 block konnyaku (devil's tongue jelly)

Simmering stock
2 Tbsp dashi stock
1 Tbsp mirin
1 Tbsp light soy sauce

Tofu dressing
1/2 block firm tofu / 4 Tbsp toasted sesame (white) / 2/3 Tbsp sake / 1 1/2 Tbsp sugar / 1/2 Tbsp light soy sauce / Dash salt

PREPARATION

■Tofu
① Wrap in a thick dish towel and then roll in a bamboo mat.
② Put between boards and place a weight on top. Tilt in a flat container to drain off water. Keep in the refrigerator for 2~3 hours until it is half as thick.

■Carrot, Shiitake, Konnyaku
① Cut the carrot into sticks, 1 1/4" (3 cm) long. Soak the shiitake in water until soft. Remove stems and slices.
② Place the konnyaku into water and bring it to a boil. Cook 5 minutes and transfer to cold water. Cut into sticks, 1 1/4" (3 cm) long.
③ Bring the simmering stock to a boil in a small pan. Add the vegetables and konnyaku. Cook over medium heat, stirring with chopsticks, until the liquid has been absorbed.
④ Spread in a bamboo colander and allow to stand until completely cooled.

*Ingredients good for su-miso: Scallions or nobiru (wild rocamboles) with seafood.

METHOD

1. Strain the tofu.

Soak the mesh of a strainer in water for a while and drain. Place the tofu on the mesh and press it through with a wooden spatula, moving from right and left towards you as pictured.

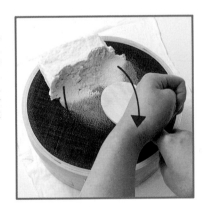

2. Mix with the sesame seeds.

Grind the toasted sesame seeds in an earthenware mortar until oil oozes. Add the sieved tofu and mix well until smooth.

3. Add the seasonings.

Add the seasonings one by one and mix well to make the tofu dressing.

4. Add the ingredients.

Combine the completely cooled carrot, shiitake and konnyaku. Mix well with the wooden spatula, which is more efficient than chopsticks.

*Ingredients good for tofu dressing: Warabi (bracken), zenmai, shungiku, seri (Japanese parsley) and fruit such as persimmon and papaya. Hijiki seaweed is also good.

SPINACH WITH SESAME DRESSING
Horenso no goma-ae

TIPS

1. Boil the spinach, several stalks at a time.
2. Toast the sesame seeds over low heat with the pan moving continually.

INGREDIENTS

5 1/4 oz (150 g) spinach
1/2 tsp light soy sauce

Sesame dressing

4 Tbsp white sesame / 1 Tbsp sugar / 1 Tbsp sake /
1/2 Tbsp soy sauce

PREPARATION

■Spinach

① Cut off the roots and wash in water.
② Divide into two parts and parboil each in ample water with a dash of salt added. First immerse the bases and then leaves.
③ Turn over immediately with chopsticks and transfer to cold water.
④ Squeeze out the water and sprinkle with light soy sauce. Let stand for a while (*Shoyu-arai).
⑤ Cut into 3/4" (2 cm) lengths and squeeze out the water again.

METHOD

1. Toast the sesame seeds.

Toast the sesame seeds over low heat in a small pan, moving continually, until you can crush a grain with the finger tips. Take care not to burn.

Low heat

2. Grind the sesame seeds and season.

Spread a wet dishtowel under an earthenware mortar to steady it. Grind the toasted sesame seeds. Hold the pestle lightly with the right hand and move circularly with the left hand.

Grind well until oil exudes and add the seasonings one by one. Mix well until smooth.

3. Add the spinach.

Add the spinach and dress it with the sesame dressing. If a wooden spatula and chopsticks are used, the spinach will be well dressed.

*Shoyu-arai: This method is to sprinkle a few drops of soy sauce over parboiled ingredients to avoid a watery taste and season lightly.

STRING BEANS WITH SESAME DRESSING

Ingen no goma-yogoshi

This dish is called 'goma-yogoshi' (dish smeared with black sesame seeds).

TIPS

1. Don't transfer the string beans into cold water after parboiling.
2. Grind the sesame seeds while hot.

INGREDIENTS

3 1/2 oz (100 g) string beans
1 tsp light soy sauce

Sesame dressing
4 Tbsp black sesame / 1 Tbsp sugar / 1 Tbsp sake /
1/2 Tbsp soy sauce

PREPARATION

① Remove strings from the string beans and parboil in lightly salted water, about 1 minute after it comes to a boil, until tender.
② Transfer to a bamboo colander and fan to cool. Cut into 3/4" (2 cm) lengths and sprinkle with light soy sauce.

METHOD

Toast the sesame seeds over low heat and grind while hot in an earthenware mortar until sticky. Add the seasonings and mix well until smooth. Add the string beans and dress them with the sesame dressing.

*Ingredients good for sesame dressing: Cucumber and briefly parboiled eggplant.

RAPE BLOSSOMS DRESSED IN SOY SAUCE WITH MUSTARD

Nanohana no karashi-joyu

TIP

Dissolve the mustard in lukewarm water (105°F / 40°C). When dissolved in cold water, it loses spiciness, and in hot water, it becomes too spicy.

INGREDIENTS

1/2 bunch rape blossoms

Soy sauce with mustard
1 tsp dissolved mustard / 1/2 Tbsp sake / 1 Tbsp light soy sauce

PREPARATION

① Wash the rape blossoms well in water and cut off the hard parts near the roots.
② Parboil in lightly salted water, three stalks at a time. Transfer to cold water.
③ Bring together in water, remove and squeeze the water out. Cut into bite-sized pieces and chill.

METHOD

Add the soy sauce and sake to the dissolved mustard and mix well. Add the rape blossoms and dress them with the mustard mixture.

*Ingredients good for soy sauce with mustard: Wakame and cucumber.

SOY-STEEPED SPINACH

Horenso no ohitashi

TIPS

1. Parboil 2~3 stalks at a time to keep them a little tough.
2. Squeeze the water out completely and the soy dressing lightly.

INGREDIENTS

5 1/4 oz (150 g) spinach
Bonito flakes

Soy dressing
3/4 cup dashi stock / 1 1/2 Tbsp light soy sauce

PREPARATION

Trim off the spinach roots and cut a cross into the base of thick stems to boil evenly.

Soak in water for a while and then wash from side to side in a bowl. Remove any dirt in the roots under running water.

Divide into two parts, and parboil each separately, stems first, in ample lightly salted water.

When the leaves sink, hold the roots and turn over. When turned over, the spinach is almost done.

Plunge immediately into cold water and parboil the other part in the same way. Holding the stems, arrange the whole under water and take out to squeeze out the excess water.

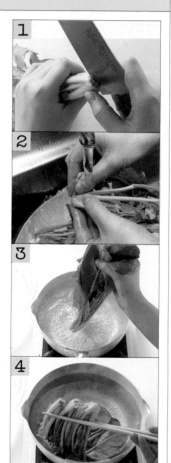

TO SERVE

Heap the spinach in bowls and top with bonito flakes. Pour the dressing from the side.

METHOD

1. Soak in the soy dressing.

Combine the dashi stock and soy sauce in a flat container and soak the spinach. Keep in the refrigerator for about 20 minutes until seasoned well before serving.

2. Squeeze out the liquid and cut.

Squeeze lightly so that a little liquid remains. First, cut in half and align the top of leaves and the roots. Cut in half and cut again into bite-sized lengths.

*Ingredients good for soy dressing: Leafy vegetables such as komatsuna, Japanese parsley, mitsuba (honewort) and daikon radish sprouts.

SOY-STEEPED MITSUBA

Ne-mitsuba no ohitashi

TIPS
1. Boil the leaves and stems separately.
2. Tie the leaves and stems before boiling.

INGREDIENTS

5 1/4 oz (150 g) mitsuba (honewort)   3/4 cup dashi stock
Crushed nori seaweed   2 Tbsp light soy sauce

PREPARATION

① Cut off the roots of mitsuba and wash in water. Cut in half and separate the leaves from the stems. Tie each with a stem.
② Parboil the leaves and stems separately in ample lightly salted water. Transfer to cold water and drain.

METHOD

Combine the dashi stock and soy sauce in a flat container. Soak the mitsuba and keep in the refrigerator for about 20 minutes. Cut into bite-sized pieces. Top with crumbled nori and pour the soy dressing over.

SOY-STEEPED ASPARAGUS AND SHIITAKE

Asupara to shiitake no yaki-bitashi

TIPS
1. Grill the asparagus until just tender.
2. Plunge the hot ingredients into the soy dressing.

INGREDIENTS

4 green asparagus   1/2 cup dashi stock
4 fresh shiitake mushrooms 1 1/2 Tbsp light soy sauce

PREPARATION

① Cut off the hard part near the root of asparagus. You may break one and, using it as a measure, cut the other together in the same lengths.
② Scrape off the outer skin and cut into half.
③ Remove dirt from the shiitake with a wet dishtowel. Cut off the stems.

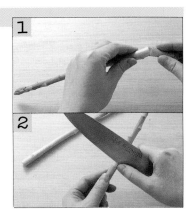

METHOD

Heat the gridiron and grill the asparagus and shiitake over medium heat until aromatic. Soak them in the mixture of the dashi stock and soy sauce. Cut into bite-sized pieces. Serve while hot or after cooled.

*Make use of the mitsuba root: Scrape off the fine root and use for kimpira (see page 29).

TIPS FOR VINEGARED AND DRESSED DISHES

Use fresh ingredients.

The vinegared and dressed dishes use fresh or briefly cooked seafood or vegetables, and the taste depends on their quality. Try to select the fresh ingredients possible. These dishes use the ingredients raw or lightly cooked, so carefully wash and drain completely.

Parboiled vegetables like spinach are sprinkled with a dash of soy sauce after the excess water is squeezed out.

Prepare before other dishes.

Deep-fried and broiled dishes are served hot, but vinegared and dressed dishes are served cold.

Accordingly, prepare them ahead of other items and keep the prepared ingredients in the refrigerator together with the dressing.

Don't forget to chill the containers at the same time.

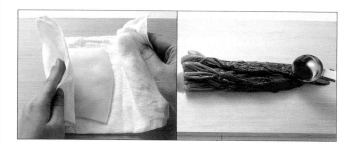

Dress just before serving.

If dressed dishes are kept long, they lose the taste, become watery and the color deteriorates. Drain the cooled ingredients again and dress just before serving.

Vinegared dressing like nihai-zu and sanbai-zu, should be poured around the side of heaped ingredients.

Seasoning changes according to the purpose and seasons.

Slightly sweet dishes are good for cooked rice. Dishes, which are less sweet and plain, go well with alcoholic drinks.

Dishes, which have an acid taste, are suitable for spring and summer, and those with less acidity for autumn and winter.

It is important to keep in mind that the adjustment of seasoning brings out savory taste.

Variations of serving.

The same ingredients give different feeling when the serving methods change. If the use of dressing changes, the display also changes as pictured below. Try and work out your own serving methods.

Coat with dressing

Top with dressing

Place ingredients on dressing

SASHIMI DISHES

Sashimi

SASHIMI
Sashimi

Sashimi, sliced raw fish, is a unique feature of Japanese cuisine. Choose fresh seasonal fish and cut with a sharp knife.

TIPS
1. Hold the fish with tips of fingers of the left hand so as not to convey heat.
2. Prepare plenty of ice for ken and tsuma.

TO SERVE
Ken, which is the bed of finely shredded daikon radish; tsuma, which includes myoga-take; and ao-tosaka are placed farthest away from you. Place the aojiso between the ken and tuna and between tuna and sea bream and squid. Arrange other sashimi attractively as shown in the photo and garnish with the bofu and kahojiso. Place the wasabi on a stand of cucumber (see p. 153).

INGREDIENTS

5 1/4 oz (150 g) tuna fillet
5 1/4 oz (150 g) sea bream
5 1/4 oz (150 g) squid
3 1/2 oz (100 g) cuttlefish
Kimi-soboro (sieved hard-cooked egg yellow)
Ao-tosaka (green seaweed), kahojiso (shiso seed pods), bofu (a kind of Japanese parsley), and murame (buds of red beefsteak plant)
Grated wasabi

Toasted nori
2" (5 cm) daikon radish
1/2 cucumber
6 myoga-take (young stem of Japanese ginger)
4 aojiso (green shiso leaves)

ASSORTMENT OF SASHIMI

*Otsukuri: In the Kansai area, the word 'sashimi' is avoided because it literally means 'spear the body.' Instead 'otsukuri' (make up) is used.

Flat-cut Tuna

Square-cut Tuna

Flat-cut Sea Bream

Slant-cut Sea Bream

Strips of Squid

Rolled Cuttlefish

PREPARATION

1. Tsuma and ken.

■Daikon radish

① Cut into 2" (5 cm) lengths. Peel thinly all the way around. Roll the daikon with one hand to peel a long, continuous strip(katsura-muki).
② Roll the thin daikon sheet into the original shape.
③ Slice thinly across the roll and soak in ice water.

■Myoga-take

Remove both ends and cut in half lengthwise. Cut diagonally into thin slices and put into ice water.

■Ao-tosaka

Wash away salt and soak in water for 7~8 minutes. Remove the hard tips of the stems and tear into bite-sized pieces.

■Cucumber

Cut into 2" (5 cm) lengths and peel. Peel thinly all the way around as far as the core into a long, continuous strip. Roll up together with the core and cut into thin slices and put into ice water.

Katsura-muki

Mizutama-kyuri

2. Grate the wasabi just before serving.

Grate before serving to retain the pungent aroma. Discard the stem and peel from the top end.

Using a fine grater, start grating from the leafy end, not from the root, and move the stalk against the grater in a circular motion. Shark skin graters are best.

Powdered wasabi

Powdered wasabi is convenient but inferior in flavor. It is hard to mix with soy sauce. To prepare it, mix it with grated daikon radish instead of water, and the mixture will be as soft as fresh wasabi.

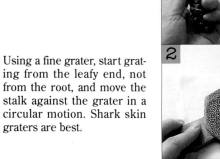

VARIATIONS OF KEN

A Aka-tosaka
B Shiro-tosaka
C Wakame
D Ao-tosaka
E Myoga-take
F Shiraga-negi
G Mizutama-kyuri
H Shiraga-daikon

Tosaka: Soak in water for 7~8 minutes to remove salt. Discard the hard tips of the stems and tear into bite-sized pieces. **Wakame**: See page 35. **Shiraga-negi**: See page 12. Wrap in cheesecloth and place under running water.

VARIATIONS OF TSUMA

A Aojiso
B Myoga
C Kahojiso
D Bakudaikai
E Kiku-nori
F Bofu
G Suizenji-nori
H Murame
I Benitade
J Me-negi
K Akaito-nori
L Hari-ninjin
M Yori-udo

Bakudaikai and **Suizenji-nori**: See page 115. **Kiku-nori**: See page 115. **Yori-udo**: Peel thinly all the way around the udo. Cut diagonally into 1/4" (5 mm) widths and put into ice water for a while.

METHOD

Flat-cut Tuna

Lay the block of tuna fillet horizontally on a cutting board. Decide the thickness with the thumb of left hand, and draw the knife swiftly towards you. At each cut, separate the slice and push over sideways.

Square-cut Tuna

Cut the block of tuna fillet (1/2 × 1 1/4"(1.5 × 3 cm)) into a bar, about 4" (10 cm) long. Thread with a bamboo skewer, dip in boiling water and transfer to ice water. Pat dry and cut into pieces, about 3/8" (1 cm) thick.

Flat-cut Sea Bream

Lay the block of sea bream fillet horizontally with the thick part farther away from you. Decide the thickness with the thumb of left hand, and draw the knife swiftly towards you. After each cut, separate the slice and push over sideways.

Slant-cut Sea Bream

Lay the fish diagonally with the skin side upwards. Cut diagonally from the left side. After each cut, separate the slice and push over sideways with the left hand.

Strips of Squid

Prepare the squid as shown on page 155. Cut it sideways. Dip in boiling water quickly and transfer to ice water. Pat dry and lay horizontally on a cutting board. Holding the knife at a sharp angle, cut it into strips, about 1/4" (5 mm) thick.

Rolled Cuttlefish

Dip the cuttlefish in boiling water and transfer to ice water. Pat dry and cut into half sideways. Lay on plastic wrap and top with nori seaweed, shorter than the fish by 3/8" (1 cm). Roll up and twist both ends of the wrap. Cut into pieces, 3/8" (1 cm) wide.

HAKATA-STYLE CUTTLEFISH

This sashimi looks like the patterns of Hakata-obi sash. Dip the cuttlefish in boiling water, transfer to ice water and pat dry. Cut in half horizontally and sandwich nori seaweed in between. Cut into 3/8" (1cm) wide.

GO-STYLE CUTTLEFISH

It looks like black and white go stones. Dip the cuttlefish in boiling water, transfer to ice water and pat dry. Cut in half horizontally, place nori on top. Make scores at intervals of 3/8" (1 cm). Cut into pieces about 3/8" (1 cm) wide.

VINEGARED MACKEREL

Shime-saba

TIP
Sprinkle ample salt over the fish and soak in vinegar as long as desired.

TO SERVE
Place tsuma of myoga-take and naganegi in the back and stand a piece of aojiso between them and the fish. Garnish with bofu and benitade and put a dab of mustard paste on the side.

INGREDIENTS

1/2 mackerel, 10 1/2 oz (300 g)
5 Tbsp salt
Vinegar
3 myoga-take (young stem of Japanese ginger)

1/2 naganegi (Japanese bunching onion)
2 aojiso (green shiso leaves)
Bofu (a kind of Japanese parsley)
Benitade (red smartweed)
Prepared mustard

PREPARATION

■Mackerel
① See page 154 for cutting the fish into three fillets. Cut off the bones on the belly side. Sprinkle ample salt over. Cover with plastic wrap and keep in the refrigerator overnight.
② Rinse quickly in water and pat dry. Place in a flat container and cover with vinegar and let stand for 40 minutes to 2 hours.
③ Pick out bones in the middle.
④ Remove the skin from the head side.

■Myoga-take
Rinse in water and cut off both ends. Cut in half lengthwise and cut diagonally into thin slices. Place in ice water and then drain.

■Naganegi
Cut into 1 1/2" (4 cm) lengths. Make a score lengthwise and remove the core. Cut into julienne strips. Wrap in cheesecloth and rub under running water (Shiraga-negi, p.12).

■Aojiso, Bofu
Rinse quickly in water and drain completely.

METHOD

1. Separate the back and belly and remove the dark-flesh.
Cut the fish lengthwise and separate the back and belly. Remove the dark-flesh of bloody color. If the fish is small, you need not remove the dark-flesh.

2. Slice into 1/4" (7 mm) thickness.

Lay the fish horizontally with the thick part farther away. Draw the knife and slice into 1/4" (7 mm) thickness.

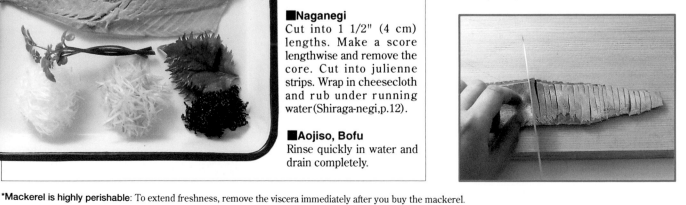

*Mackerel is highly perishable: To extend freshness, remove the viscera immediately after you buy the mackerel.

CHOPPED HORSE MACKEREL
Aji no tataki

TIPS

1. Season the fish lightly and mix with the condiments.
2. Chill completely.

TO SERVE

Place 2 aojiso on a plate and heap the ingredients on the leaves with the sudachi beside.

INGREDIENTS

1 horse mackerel, 7 oz (200 g)	1 tsp sake
8 aojiso (green shiso leaves)	2 tsp soy sauce
1 clove ginger root	1 tsp hatcho-miso
1/2 bunch chives	1 sudachi (citrus fruit)

PREPARATION

■Horse mackerel

See page 154 for cutting the fish into three fillets.

① Insert the knife underneath the pectoral fin, sever the head and remove the innards. Rinse quickly under water and pat dry.

② Cut into three fillets and remove the backbone. Running fingers along the fillets. remove remaining bones.

③ Peel the skin from the head side. If you smear vinegar on the skin, you can easily peel.

■Aojiso

Set aside four leaves for placing under the fish. Cut the other four leaves into julienne strips. Immerse in water to remove the harshness and squeeze water out.

■Ginger, Chives

Chop the ginger and cut the chives crosswise into thin pieces.

METHOD

1. Slice the horse mackerel and season lightly.

Cut the fish into slices about 1/4" (5 mm) thick. Pour the sake and soy sauce over lightly.

2. Chop miso and condiments together.

Put the miso, aojiso, ginger and chives on the fish. Chop the whole, mixing.

*Hatcho-miso: Main materials are soybeans and salt. This savory miso is rich in taste.

TIPS FOR SASHIMI DISHES

Ken, Tsuma, Karami

Ken (p. 82), tsuma (p. 82) and karami (pungent condiment) are three indispensable ingredients for sashimi. They are not decorations. They are used to get rid of fishy smell, bring out the taste and color and help digestion. Ken is fine strips of daikon radish, cucumber or seaweed, which are put to the side or placed under the sashimi. Tsuma includes benitade (red smartweed), aojiso (green shiso leaves) and hojiso (ears of perilla), which make the sashimi colorful and add flavor. Karami gives a pungent taste and prevents poisoning.

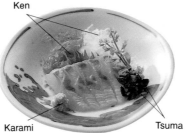

Ken
Karami
Tsuma

How to cut sashimi

The preparation of sashimi is very simple. Just cut fresh raw seafood into bite-sized pieces. The taste, however, depends on the skill of cutting.
Use a sharp knife, preferably a sashimi-knife. Lay the fillet on the front part of cutting board.
Start with the heel of the knife and draw it towards you in one stroke, making use of the weight of the knife.

A variation of karami

The most popular condiment is wasabi horseradish, but some other condiments are used according to the type of sashimi.

■Grated ginger

Used for the sashimi of mackerel, horse mackerel, sardine and cuttlefish.

■Dissolved mustard

Always used for vinegared mackerel.

■Chopped ume flesh

Used for the sashimi of whitefish in summer. In the Kansai area, it accompanies sea-eel.

■Others

Grated garlic for chopped bonito and momiji-oroshi (grated daikon with red chili pepper) for globefish. A combination of wasabi and chopped ume flesh is also used.

Soy sauce for dipping

Koikuchi or regular soy sauce is generally used for sashimi, but there are several other kinds of soy sauce. Some people prefer tamari-joyu and kanro-joyu, which are darker and thicker soy sauce, as the dipping sauce. Tosa-joyu and kagen-joyu are also popular.
To make tosa-joyu, bring to a boil; 1 cup of soy sauce with 1 Tbsp each of mirin and sake and 3/8 oz (10 g) bonito flakes. Boil down over medium heat until about 10% reduced. Let stand to cool and strain through cheesecloth.
Kagen-joyu is light soy sauce combined with the same quantity of dashi stock.

Arrange to match containers.

ROUND PLATE

Place ken at the back and sashimi in the center. Arrange tsuma and karami well balanced in front.

BOWL

Arrange in the same way as the round plate. Since the container is deep, collect all in a heap in the center.

SQUARE PLATE

Place types of sashimi separately. When they are of the same fish, cut each differently as shown in the photo.

ONE POT
DISHES

Nabemono

ASSORTED CASSEROLE

Yose-nabe

Cooked at the table, casserole dishes are a real treat in cold weather. Using a great variety of materials, this dish is gorgeous and nourishing. You may add many kinds of condiments to suit your taste.

TIPS

1. Have everything you need on the table before starting cooking.
2. Season the cooking liquid lightly as it is eaten. Avoid putting too much in the pot at one time.
3. Eat what is cooked immediately while hot.

INGREDIENTS

8 clams
1/2 kinmedai (alfonsino), 14 oz (400 g)
7 oz (200 g) chicken thigh
1 3/4 oz (50 g) harusame (starch noodles)
6 leaves Chinese cabbage, 21 oz (600 g)
2 7/8 oz (80 g) spinach
7 oz (200 g) daikon radish
1 3/4 oz (50 g) carrot
2 naganegi (Japanese bunching onion)
8 fresh shiitake mushrooms
10 1/2" (300g) shungiku (edible leafy chrysanthemum)

Cooking broth
9 cups dashi stock / 1 Tbsp salt / 3 Tbsp light soy sauce / 3 Tbsp sake

PREPARATION

■Clams
Use only those which give a clear sound when hit together. Remove those which give a dull sound, because they are dead. Wash with a brush under running water.

■Harusame
Place in a large bowl and pour boiling water over. Allow to stand until they become transparent. Plunge in cold water, drain and cut into bite-sized lengths.

■Spinach rolled up in Chinese cabbage
① Slide Chinese cabbage leaves one by one into salted boiling water. When they become soft, plunge in cold water. Parboil the spinach and also plunge in cold water. Squeeze the excess water out of both.
② Lay two Chinese cabbage leaves on the bamboo mat, the leafy parts overlapping the stalks of the other. Place 1/3 of the spinach on top.
③ Roll up using the bamboo mat. Form the shape of the roll and squeeze out the excess water again.
④ Do the same with the other Chinese cabbage leaves and spinach and make three rolls in all. Cut into 1 1/4" (3 cm) pieces.

■Kinmedai
This is oily white fish. Cut into bite-sized chunks. Arrange in a bamboo colander and sprinkle with salt. Pour boiling water over and then ice water quickly. Cook the head and innards together, if available.

■Chicken thigh
Remove yellow fat and excess skin. Cut in half lengthwise and then into bite-sized pieces.

■Daikon, Carrot
Cut half of the daikon and carrot into slices about 1/8" (3~4 mm) thick. Using a cookie cutter, make into a shape of twisted plum blossom (see p. 153). Parboil quickly in boiling water. Cut the other daikon and carrot into julienne strips about 2" (5 cm) long.

■Naganegi, Shiitake, Shungiku
Cut the naganegi diagonally into pieces about 1/4" (5 mm) thick. Wipe dirt from the caps of shiitake mushrooms with wet dish-cloth and cut off the stems. Cut off the root and hard part near the root of shungiku and rinse in water.

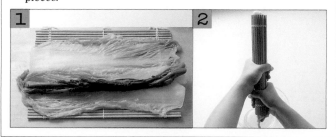

*Yose-nabe: Materials used differ according to regions. Kanto area uses more seafood and Kansai area add yuba (dried bean curd) and fu (wheat gluten).

1. Make light seasoning broth.
Fill an earthenware pot with the dashi stock and place it over low heat. Add salt and soy sauce to season. If the outside bottom of the earthenware pot is wet, it is liable to crack, so wipe it clean before using.

2. Start with the seafood.
Start with the seafood and chicken, which flavor the broth, and the daikon radish and carrot, which require longer cooking. When the liquid comes to a boil, remove any scum.

3. Cook the remaining ingredients.
After a while, add all the other ingredients except the shungiku, a little at a time, replenishing the pot as needed. Add the shungiku last and cook quickly before discoloring.

Low heat

SUKIYAKI

Sukiyaki

There are two kinds of sukiyaki, Kansai style and Kanto style.
Kansai style: Add condiments directly to the ingredients fried in the pan.
Kanto style: Season the ingredients with sauce called warishita.

TIP

Flavor the oil with naganegi. Don't overcook beef.

INGREDIENTS

14 oz (400 g) thin slices of beef (sirloin)
Beef suet
4 kuruma-bu*
1 block yaki-dofu (grilled tofu)
1 pack shirataki (konnyaku noodles)
3 naganegi (Japanese bunching onion)
1 bunch shungiku (edible leafy chrysanthemum)

Seasoning

3/4 cup sugar / 3/5 cup mirin / 3/4 cup soy sauce

PREPARATION

■Beef
Cut crosswise against the grain into bite-sized lengths.

■Kuruma-bu
Soak in water for 3 minutes. Squeeze the excess water out by sandwiching between palms of hands.

■Yaki-dofu
Cut into 8 portions.

■Shirataki
Place in cold water and then bring to a boil for 5 minutes. Dip in ice water and drain. Cut into bite-sized lengths.

■Naganegi, Shungiku
Slice the naganegi diagonally. Rinse the shungiku, moving from side to side. Discard the root and the hard part near the root.

METHOD

1. Melt the beef suet completely.

Heat a sukiyaki skillet (if unavailable, a frying pan will do) and melt the beef suet over low heat. Take time until the skillet is well oiled. The suet provides a richer taste than vegetable oil. You may get it at butcher's shop.

2. Start with the negi.

Add several pieces of negi and fry lightly. The negi gives flavor to the oil. Spread beef slices over the negi and cook quickly.

3. Season with condiments.

While the beef is partly red, add 3 Tbsp each of sugar, mirin and soy sauce. Add the shirataki, yaki-dofu, kuruma-bu and the remaining negi, a little at a time. Season all quickly.

*Kuruma-bu: Baked wheat gluten. There is a hole in the middle like a wheel(kuruma).

4. Add the shungiku last.

Before the beef is overcooked, add the shungiku and cook until soft. When cooked, help yourselves, if you like, dipping in beaten egg before eating.
When all is eaten, start again from 2.

When the liquid is gone:

When the liquid is reduced midway, add dashi stock or sake.

Warishita

Kanto-style warishita: Bring 3/4 cup soy sauce, 3/4 cup sugar and 1/2 cup mirin to a boil. Add about 1/2 cup dashi stock. Pre-cooked food is seasoned with the warishita.

ODEN

Oden

Oden is a popular one-pot dish. The taste improves when left overnight, so prepare a large quantity.

TIPS

1. Cook the food in another pot and transfer to earthenware to serve. It will look attractive. Strain the liquid through cheesecloth.
2. Continue adding liquid while cooking.
3. Cook over low heat. If it is kept boiling, the liquid will become cloudy.

INGREDIENTS

10 1/2 oz (300 g) daikon radish
10 1/2 oz (300 g) potatoes
1 block yaki-dofu (grilled tofu)
1/2 konnyaku (devil's tongue jelly)
2 eggs
8 cooked kombu, 6" (15 cm) long
1 grilled chikuwa (broiled fish-paste cake)
4 satsuma-age (deep-fried fish-paste cake)
8 age-boru (deep-fried dumpling)
4 small ganmodoki (deep-fried tofu containing vegetables)

Cooking broth

12 cups dashi stock / 1/3 cup sake / 1 1/3 Tbsp salt /
3 Tbsp light soy sauce

PREPARATION

■Daikon radish

① Cut into round slices about 1 1/2" (4 cm) thick and peel. Trim all around removing the 90 degree angle. This helps it to keep its shape during boiling.
② Make crisscross cuts as deep as half so as to absorb seasonings.
③ Parboil in water in which rice is washed. Rinse in lukewarm water.

■Ni-kombu

① Wipe with dry dishtowel to remove dirt. Wrap in wet paper towel and let stand until soft.
② Tie in the middle.

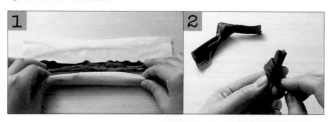

■Satsuma-age, Age-boru, Ganmodoki

The oil on the surface of deep-fried food like satsuma-age and ganmodoki is oxidized when left long after cooking. Arrange them separately in a bamboo colander and pour boiling water over to remove the excess oil.

■Konnyaku

① Cover with water and bring it to a boil. Boil for 5 minutes to make it firm and dip in water to cool.
② Make scores on the surface so as to absorb seasonings. Cut into bite-sized triangles.

■Potatoes

Pare the skin. Place the whole in water and bring it to a boil.

■Yaki-dofu, Yaki-chikuwa, Eggs

Cut the tofu and chikuwa into four equal portions. Make hard boiled eggs and shell in water.

*Chameshi: Rice cooked with light soy sauce (chameshi) is said to go well with oden.

1. Cook separately in different pans.

In a pan (8 1/4" / 21 cm), bring the dashi stock to a boil and add condiments to make the cooking broth. In a pan (9 1/2" / 24 cm), place the daikon, potatoes, konnyaku, yaki-dofu, kombu and hard-boiled eggs. Cover with the broth and bring to a boil over high heat.

2. Add the ganmodoki.

Simmer over low heat for 20 minutes, adding the broth when it is reduced. Add the ganmodoki and simmer for another 20 minutes.

Low heat

3. Add the deep-fried food last.

Add the chikuwa, satsuma-age and age-boru last. They are ready when warmed up. Don't overcook them.

4. Transfer to the earthenware pot.

Arrange the food colorfully in the earthenware pot, which is placed over the lowest heat. Add the cooking broth, straining through cheesecloth. Help yourselves according to individual preferences.

TIPS FOR ONE POT DISHES

Cook a little at a time.

In the case of yose-nabe and sukiyaki, which are cooked at the table, avoid putting too much in the pot at once. It takes time for the food to be done and the food will be overcooked while eating. Match the pace of adding things to that of those eating.

Prepare a vessel for bones and shells.

In the case of seafood dishes, prepare a vessel at the table to put cast-off bones and shells in. If they are left on the platter, they look unpleasant.

Carefully remove the scum.

In any cooking, it is important to skim off any scum that forms midway. The well-seasoned broth of Yose-nabe is eaten together with the food, so remove the scum carefully.

Use ample condiments.

For lightly seasoned dishes, use a variety of condiments as desired. It is enjoyable to make your own taste by combining them.

A Yuzu (citrus) strips
B Yuzu
C Chives
D Grated daikon radish
E Momiji-oroshi (p.152)

The pleasure after cooking

Making use of the well-seasoned broth, you can make rice porridge or cook noodles and rice cakes.

Rice porridge with eggs (photo: ①~④)

① Scoop out the remaining bones and ingredients.
② Wash cooked rice in a colander and separate the grains. Place in boiling broth and bring to a boil.
③ Scatter chopped chives over. Pour beaten eggs over and turn off the heat immediately.
④ Cover with a lid until the eggs are soft-boiled.

RICE AND NOODLES

Gohan / Men

MIXED SUSHI

Chirashi-zushi

TIPS
1. All other ingredients should be prepared before cooking rice.
2. After vinegar mixture is poured over the rice, let it stand a while.

INGREDIENTS (4 servings)　　　　　　　　　　　*Prepare cooked rice more than needed.

■Fillings

2 eggs
1 tsp sugar
Dash salt
Vegetable oil

12 dried shiitake mushrooms
1 cup dashi stock
4 Tbsp sugar
2 Tbsp each of mirin and soy sauce

3 1/2 oz (100 g) lotus root
2 Tbsp dashi stock
2 Tbsp vinegar
1 Tbsp sugar
Dash salt

12 shrimp
2 Tbsp dashi stock
1 Tbsp vinegar
1/2 Tbsp sugar
Dash salt

20 (9"/23 cm long) kampyo (dried gourd strips)
1 1/2 cups dashi stock
4 Tbsp each of sugar, mirin and soy sauce

1 3/4 oz (50 g) carrot
1/2 tsp vinegar
1 tsp sugar
Dash salt

1 3/4 oz (50 g) snow peas
1/2 cup white sesame seeds
1 toasted nori
20 kinome (young leaves of prickly ash)

■Sushi rice
4 cups rice
4 cups water
1 piece kombu kelp, 4" (10 cm) square

Vinegar mixture
1/2 cup vinegar
4 1/2 Tbsp sugar
1 tsp salt

PREPARATION (Fillings)

■Kinshi-tamago*
Break eggs into a bowl. Stir with chopsticks, cutting whites but do not beat. Add seasonings and strain through a sieve. Heat an oiled frying pan and make 3 thin omelets. Place on a turned-over bamboo colander to cool. Cut in half and roll up. Cut the rolls into julienne strips.

■Dried shiitake mushrooms
Rinse quickly and soak in water. Cut off the hard tips. Cook in the dashi stock with sugar, skimming the scum, for 4~5 minutes. Add mirin and soy sauce and simmer over medium heat until the liquid is completely gone. Transfer to a flat container to cool. Discard the stems and cut into thin slices.

■Lotus root
Pare and soak in vinegared water. Cut into thin slices and then soak in vinegared water again for 3 minutes. Parboil quickly in boiling water. Immerse in the dashi stock and seasonings and let stand until cooled.

■Snow peas
Remove strings and parboil in salted water. Cut diagonally into thin strips.

■Shrimp
Devein with a bamboo skewer. Parboil in salted water until the color changes to vivid red. Transfer to a bamboo colander to cool. Cut off the head and tail and shell. Immerse in the dashi stock and seasonings.

■Kampyo
Reconstitute kampyo as described on page 35. Cook in the dashi stock and sugar over low heat about 5 minutes. Add the mirin and soy sauce and simmer over medium heat until the liquid is almost gone. Transfer to a flat container to cool. Cut into pieces, 3/8" (1 cm) long.

■Carrot
Pare and cut into julienne strips, 1 1/4" (3 cm) long. Place in a small pan and cover with water. Add seasonings and simmer over medium heat, occasionally stirring, until the liquid is almost gone. Transfer to a flat container to cool.

■White sesame seeds, Toasted nori, Kinome
Toast the sesame seeds until aromatic. Tear the nori and crumple. Rinse the kinome quickly.

*Kinshi-tamago: Shredded thin omelet, which literally means 'golden thread eggs.'

PREPARATION (Sushi rice)

① Wash the rice quickly an hour before cooking. Adjust the quantity of water and let stand. When ready to cook, wipe dirt from the kombu (kelp) with dry cheesecloth. Put it in the rice and start cooking.

② When it comes to a boil, remove the kombu. If it remains longer, it will absorb the water, resulting in firm cooked rice.

③ When cooked, leave the rice to steam for 7~8 minutes. Transfer the rice in one stroke to a wooden tub, which is moistened with vinegared water. Pour the vinegar mixture over the rice.

④ Level the rice off with a paddle and spread the vinegar mixture all over.

⑤ Allow to stand a while. With vertical cutting movements of the paddle, mix thoroughly. While mixing, fan the rice with a hand fan.

⑥ Gather the rice to the middle of the tub using cheesecloth moistened with vinegared water. Don't leave any grains around the mound as shown in the photo.

METHOD

When the rice is cooled to body temperature, scatter the materials over, starting from dry ingredients, in the order of sesame seeds, nori, shiitake, kampyo, carrot and snow peas.

Turning the tub around, mix the materials in the front a little at a time. Mix the whole together last.

TO SERVE

Heap up the rice mixture on a plate and scatter the kinshi-tamago over. Garnish colorfully with the lotus root, shrimp and kinome.

THICK SUSHI ROLLS
Futomaki-zushi

TO SERVE
The finished end of the nori faces toward you.

Use one and a half sheets of nori to make voluminous rolls. You will feel full with just one roll.

TIPS
1. Start rolling after the rice is cooled to body temperature.
2. Make grooves at equal intervals so that the fillings come in the center.

INGREDIENTS (For 3 rolls)

■ Fillings
8 dry shiitake mushrooms
3/4 cup dashi stock
3 Tbsp sugar
1 1/2 Tbsp each of mirin and soy sauce

12 (9"/23 cm long) kampyo (dried gourd strips)
1 cup dashi stock
3 Tbsp sugar
2 Tbsp each of mirin and soy sauce

2 small bunches mitsuba (honewort)
1 3/4 oz (50 g) umezu-shoga (sweet-vinegared ginger)

5 eggs
3 Tbsp sugar
Dash salt
Vegetable oil

■ Sushi rice
4 cups rice
4 cups water
1 kombu kelp, 4"(10 cm) square

Vinegar mixture
1/2 cup vinegar
5 Tbsp sugar
1 tsp salt

4 1/2 sheets toasted nori

PREPARATION

■Fillings
Cook the shiitake and kampyo as directed on page 96. Cut off the stems of the shiitake and cut into thin slices. Align the kampyo. Parboil the mitsuba quickly. Cut the umezu-shoga into 1/4" (5 mm) sticks. Break the eggs and stir. Add seasonings to the eggs and strain. Make thick omelet (see p. 46). Cut into three equal portions.

■Sushi rice
Cook as directed on page 97. Start rolling when it is cooled to body temperature.

METHOD

1. Join one sheet and a half sheet of nori.

Place a bamboo mat with the skin side up. Lay a sheet of nori with shiny side down on the mat. Join the half sheet using three grains of rice as glue.

2. Spread the rice evenly.

Place 1/3 of the rice a little below the middle. Spread it over, leaving about 3/4" (2 cm) space at the far edge.

3. Make grooves and put fillings in.

Make a groove at 1 1/4" (3 cm) from the end nearest you. Make three more grooves at 1 1/4" (3 cm) intervals so that the fillings come in the center when rolled. Beginning at the side closest to you, lay the fillings in the grooves in the following order; kampyo, shiitake, omelet and umezu-shoga and mitsuba.

4. Bring the edge of the bamboo mat over to the other end.

Pick up the corners of the edge of the mat together with the nori, lightly pressing the kampyo with the middle fingers. Starting with the kampyo bring the whole to join at the other end.

5. Shape the whole and flatten both ends.

Place the joint of the nori down and hold the whole tightly with both hands to shape.

Next holding the roll with the right hand, use the left hand to pull the mat away to tighten roll and shape.

Move the roll to the end of the mat. Flatten the edge, pressing with a hand moistened with vinegared water. Flatten both ends.

6. Cut into eight equal slices.

With a knife moistened with vinegared water, cut the roll into eight equal slices from the end. Wet the knife before each cut.

*The front and back of nori: The shiny surface is the front side. When rolling the sushi, the shiny side comes outside.

STUFFED TOFU PUFF SUSHI

Inari-zushi

TIPS

1. Add soy sauce to aburage after it is cooked with sugar.
2. Cook the aburage until the liquid is completely gone.
3. Cook sushi rice after the aburage is ready.

TO SERVE

Arrange with the mouth down and garnish with umezu-shoga to cleanse the palate.

INGREDIENTS (10 pieces)

5 aburage (deep-fried tofu)
1 1/2 cups dashi stock
4 Tbsp sugar
2 1/2 Tbsp mirin
2 Tbsp soy sauce

3 Tbsp white sesame seeds
Umezu-shoga (sweet-vinegared ginger)

■Sushi rice
2 cups rice
2 cups water
1 kombu kelp, 2 3/4" (7 cm) square
Vinegar mixture
1/4 cup vinegar
2 1/2 Tbsp sugar
2/3 tsp salt

PREPARATION

■**Aburage**
① Place on a cutting board vertically. Roll a long chopstick over to make it open easily.
② Cut in half crosswise. Carefully open and make a pouch.
③ Place on a bamboo colander evenly. Pour boiling water over the front and back to remove the excess oil.
④ Bring the dashi stock to a boil and add the aburage. Add the sugar and simmer over medium heat for 3~4 minutes.
⑤ Add the mirin and soy sauce. Place a small lid directly on the food and cook until the liquid is almost reduced.
⑥ Press the lid and continue cooking until the remaining liquid is completely gone. Transfer to a flat container to cool.
■**White sesame seeds**
Place in a small pan over low heat and toast, continuously moving, until aromatic.
■**Umezu-shoga**
Cut into thin slices.
■**Sushi rice**
Cook as directed on page 97 and cool to body temperature.

METHOD

1. Mix the sesame seeds with the sushi rice.

Scatter the sesame seeds over the rice and then mix. Make ten barrel shaped balls.

2. Stuff the rice.

Fold the mouth of the aburage back, 1/3 from the edge and stuff with the rice. Using thumbs, stuff the rice tightly to each corner of the pouch. Fold the edges over the pouch and shape.

*Fillings of inari-zushi: Fine strips of aojiso, kiku-nori (p.115), chirimenjako (dried young sardines), walnut, seeds of pine and hemp.

RED BEAN RICE

Okowa

This is traditional rice for auspicious occasions. Introduced here is a simple method of cooking instead of steaming.

TIP

With a fan cool the liquid in which cowpeas are cooked and the cooked rice to bring out the bright color.

TO SERVE

Sprinkle black sesame seeds over and garnish with nandin leaves.

INGREDIENTS (4 servings)

3 cups glutinous rice
1/2 cup cowpeas
Toasted sesame seeds (black)

PREPARATION

■Cowpeas
① Wash. Add 1 1/2 cups of water and cook over high heat. When it comes to a boil, add 1 1/2 cups of water. Repeat this three times, skimming the scum. Simmer for 20~25 minutes over medium heat.
② When cowpeas crush between the thumb and forefinger, turn off the heat. Separate the cowpeas and liquid. Fan the liquid to cool.

■Glutinous rice
Rub under running water and rinse until the water becomes clear. Transfer to a bamboo colander and drain.

METHOD

1. Mix the rice and cowpeas and add the liquid in which cowpeas are cooked.

Combine the rice and cowpeas and mix well. Moistened rice easily breaks so mix with great care. Place in a cooker and add the liquid in which cowpeas are cooked.

2. Adjust the water using a chopstick.

Cover with water so that it will come about 1/4" (5~6 mm) above the rice or so that a chopstick rolls over the surface. Add more water if necessary. Switch on the rice cooker. When the switch goes off, switch on again and cook twice, steaming for 10 minutes.

3. Transfer to a wooden tub and fan.

Insert a wooden spatula and move around the rice in the rice cooker. Transfer to a wooden tub in one stroke. While mixing, fan the rice with a hand fan to drive off steam and bring out glossy color.

*For mournful occasions: In the case of a mournful occasion, black beans are used to make black and white okowa.

RICE WITH VEGETABLES

Kayaku-gohan

When the harvest season of new rice arrives, we long for rice with garnishes. If possible, we would like to have a number of extra helpings.

TIPS

1. Cut all the ingredients into the same lengths so that they are cooked evenly.
2. When cooked, transfer the rice to a wooden tub to drive off steam.

INGREDIENTS (4 servings)

3 cups rice
5 dried shiitake mushrooms
1/3 block konnyaku (devil's tongue jelly)
1 3/4 oz (50 g) burdock
1 3/4 oz (50 g) carrot
1 aburage

3 1/3 cups kombu stock (see p. 109)
3 Tbsp sake
1 tsp sugar
3 Tbsp soy sauce
2/3 tsp salt

PREPARATION

■**Rice**
See page 106 for cooking. About one hour before cooking time, wash the rice quickly and soak in water and kombu stock.

■**Shiitake mushrooms**
Rinse in water and allow them to soak in ample water until soft. Discard the stems and cut the caps into thin slices.

■**Konnyaku**
Place in a small pan and cover with water. Bring it to a boil and cook for about 5 minutes until it is al dente. Dip in water to cool and drain. Cut into thin sticks, 3/4" (2 cm) long.

■**Burdock**
Wash with vegetable brush to remove dirt. Make vertical fine scores and then shave. Dip in vinegared water as soon as shaved. When the color of water changes, rinse in water and drain in a bamboo colander.

■**Carrot**
Pare and cut in the same lengths as those of konnyaku.

■**Aburage**
Place in a bamboo colander. Pour boiling water over to remove the excess oil. Cut in half and then into fine strips.

The ratio of rice and additions: Too many additions will spoil the taste. The proper quantity of the additions is half of the rice.

METHOD

1. Add the additions and seasonings to the rice.

Just before cooking, add the additions and the seasonings in this order. The rice cooker takes time before coming to a boil. If the seasonings are added earlier, the rice does not cook well, so delay adding as long as possible.

2. Mix well and dissolve the seasonings.

Mix the whole well or the seasonings will remain at the bottom, and the rice scorches and sticks to the bottom.

3. Cook twice.

When cooked in a normal way, switch on again and leave it until it switches off automatically.

4. Steam for 10 minutes.

Allow it to stand to steam for 10 minutes. The rice will not become fluffy if it is longer or shorter than 10 minutes.

5. Transfer to a wooden tub to mix.

Insert a wooden spatula and move around the rice in the rice cooker. Transfer to a moistened wooden tub or a flat container in one stroke and mix lightly. The extra water will evaporate and the rice will become fluffy.

103

NOODLES

Men-rui

BUCKWHEAT NOODLES WITH TEMPURA
(Tempura-soba)

■**Ingredients:** 9 oz (250 g) soba (buckwheat noodles) / 3 cups broth (p. 105) / 4 deep-fried shrimp / 1/4 naganegi

■**Method:** See the next page for boiling the noodles. It should be boiled al dente. Dip in boiling water. See page 50 for deep-frying the shrimp. Arrange them on top and cover with the hot broth. Garnish with thinly sliced naganegi .

WHEAT NOODLES WITH BONITO FLAKES
(Okaka-udon)

■**Ingredients:** 9 oz (250 g) udon (wheat noodles) / 3 cups broth (p. 105) / 3/16 oz (5 g) bonito flakes / 1/3 naganegi

■**Method:** See the next page for boiling the noodles. Dip in boiling water. Place in a bowl and top with naganegi (1 1/4" (3 cm) long and quartered vertically) and bonito flakes. Cover with the broth.

FINE NOODLES
(Somen)

■**Ingredients:** 7 oz (200 g) somen (fine noodles) / 1 cup broth (p. 105) / 1 clove ginger / 1 myoga / Cucumber and Kaiware (daikon sprouts)

■**Method:** See the next page for boiling the fine noodles. Dip in ice water and garnish with slices of cucumber (p. 153) and kaiware. Arrange with chilled dipping sauce, ginger and myoga as desired.

HOW TO BOIL BUCKWHEAT AND WHEAT NOODLES

1. Boil in boiling water.

Prepare a generous amount of hot water in a large pan. Bring it to a boil and add the noodles, fanning out. Stir immediately with chopsticks to prevent them from sticking together.

2. Add water.

When the water is on the point of boiling over, add 1/2 cup water. Add water again when it comes to a boil. Repeat this process as long as indicated on the packet of the noodles. Take out a noodle and eat to test the doneness.

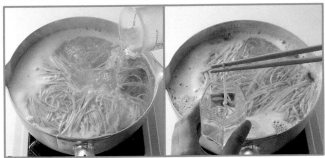

3. Transfer to a colander and squeeze.

Transfer to a colander and drain. Pour water over to cool. Set the colander in a bowl and rinse the noodles under running water, squeezing and turning with hands to get rid of stickiness. Drain.

HOW TO BOIL FINE NOODLES:

Add water once during the cooking. When it comes to a boil again, they are done. Transfer to a colander and follow the same process as directed in **(3)**

BROTH AND DIPPING SAUCE

Broth for buckwheat noodles

3 1/2 cups water / 3/4 oz (20 g) bonito and frigate mackerel flakes / 2 Tbsp sake / 3 Tbsp soy sauce / Dash salt

■Method:
① The ratio of bonito flakes and frigate mackerel flakes is 1 to 1. Combine all the ingredients in a pan and cook over high heat.
② When it comes to a boil, lower the heat. Simmer for 1~2 minutes and turn off the heat. Let stand to cool and strain through cheesecloth.

■Note: For buckwheat noodles, using only bonito flakes is not enough to make a substantial broth, so add frigate mackerel, which has strong flavor.

Dipping sauce for buckwheat noodles

1 1/2 cups water / 8 small dried sardines / 1 Tbsp sake / 1/2 Tbsp sugar / 1/2 cup mirin / 1/2 cup soy sauce

■Method:
① Gut and remove the heads of sardines. Place in a pan with water. Add the sake and let stand for an hour.
② Bring to a boil over high heat, skim off any scum and add the seasonings. Bring to a boil over medium heat and turn off. Let stand until cooled. Strain through cheesecloth.

Broth for wheat noodles

3 1/2 cups water / 1 (4 × 2"(10 × 5 cm)) kombu / 1 1/2 oz (40 g) bonito flakes / 2 Tbsp sake / 1 tsp mirin / 1 Tbsp light soy sauce /1 tsp salt

■Method:
① Wipe the kombu with dry cheesecloth. Place in a pan with water and cook over medium heat. When heated, remove the kombu. Add bonito flakes and bring to a boil. When cooled, strain through cheesecloth (see page 108).
② Bring to a boil and add the seasonings.

Dipping sauce for fine noodles

2 cups water / 1/2 oz (15 g) bonito flakes / 1/2 cup mirin / 1/2 cup light soy sauce / Dash salt

■Method:
① Place all the ingredients in a pan and bring to a boil over high heat. Lower to medium heat and cook for a minute skimming off any scum. Turn off.
② Let stand to cool until bonito flakes sink to the bottom. Chill in the refrigerator and strain through cheesecloth.

TIPS FOR RICE AND NOODLES

Washing is the key to tasty cooked rice.

Place the rice in a pan which has a flat bottom. The inside pan of a rice cooker is preferable. Prepare a generous amount of water in a bowl in advance.

Pour the water over in one motion. Water from a tap will take time and the rice will retain the bran odor.

Stir once or twice slowly. In the meantime collect water in a bowl again.

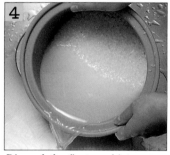

Discard the first washing water since it contains a lot of bran. If you are slow in pouring the water out, the rice will retain the bran odor.

With the finger tips, roll the rice rhythmically in one direction, rubbing the rice between the fingers and the bottom of pan.

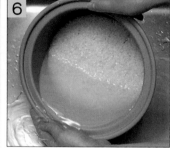

Change water 4 or 5 times until the water is clear. If you don't wash thoroughly, the cooked rice will spoil quickly.

Add a measured amount of water to the washed rice, and soak it for more than an hour so that the rice absorbs the water fully.

Transfer the rice to a wooden tub.

In making sushi rice, the rice is mixed with a vinegar mixture in a wooden tub to get rid of the extra moisture from the cooked rice. In the case of kayaku-gohan (rice with vegetables) and okowa (red bean rice), the rice and ingredients are mixed in the same way to make the rice fluffy. Some people mix them in a pot, but it is hard to mix and the steam makes the rice watery and sticky.

Vinegar mixture

The ratio of ingredients in the vinegar mixture differs according to whether making sushi rice, chirashi-zushi (mixed sushi), seafood sushi and maki-zushi (sushi rolls). Chirashi-zushi and maki-zushi use sweetened ingredients, so make the sushi rice a little sweet. Seafood sushi rice should be less sweet and plain to bring out the taste of raw ingredients.

(For 4 cups rice)	Vinegar	Sugar	Salt
Chirashi-zushi	$1/2$ cup	$4\frac{1}{2}$ Tbsp	1 tsp
Seafood sushi	$1/2$ cup	1 Tbsp	1 Tbsp
Maki-zushi	$1/2$ cup	5 Tbsp	1 tsp

SOUPS

Shirumono

DELICIOUS SOUPS depend on DASHI STOCK

DASHI STOCK OF KOMBU AND BONITO FLAKES (Ichiban Dashi)

This dashi has a savory and refreshing taste. It is widely used in Japanese cuisine for such dishes as clear and miso soups, and simmered and vinegared dishes.

Kombu good for making dashi

The best kombu comes from Hokkaido, and two varieties are well known. One is called 'ma-kombu' which is thick kelp of top quality and has a sweet flavor. Another is 'rishiri-kombu' which is black kelp.

**INGREDIENTS
(3 cups)**

3 1/2 cups water
1 piece kombu
  (4 ×2"(10×5 cm))
1 oz (30 g) bonito
  flakes

1. Remove dirt from the kombu.

Wipe off dirt and sand from the kombu with a dry cloth. Leave the white powder on the surface as it is. It is the source of the savory taste.

2. Remove just before boiling.

Place the kombu in water in a pan and cook over medium heat. When bubbles begin to come from the bottom, remove the kombu. If it is boiled for a long time, the stock will become cloudy and smelly.

Medium heat

3. Add bonito flakes.

When it comes to a boil, add bonito flakes all at once. After a short time, turn off the heat. If they are boiled for a long time, the stock will become strong-smelling.

4. Wait until the flakes sink.

Skim off any scum carefully. Let stand until the flakes sink to the bottom of the pan. If you stir, the liquid will become cloudy.

5. Strain through cheesecloth.

Place moistened and wrung out cloth over a bamboo colander. Pour the liquid over and strain. Don't squeeze the flakes but leave the liquid to drip through the cloth.

NIBAN DASHI

By making use of the ichiban flakes, you can make the niban dashi stock. It is also used as cooking liquid.

Method :

① In a pan, place the bonito flakes used for the ichiban dashi. Add 2 cups water and cook over medium heat. You may add 3/8 oz (10 g) of fresh bonito flakes to make it tastier.
② When it comes to a boil, reduce the heat and cook over low heat for 2~3 minutes. Strain in the same way as the ichiban dashi stock.

---

*Niboshi and iriko: Niboshi are small anchovies cooked in salted water and dried. The miniature variety is called iriko.

The key taste of soup depends on savory dashi stock. Dashi is also a basic cooking liquid for many other Japanese dishes. Let's master how to make good dashi stock.

IRIKO DASHI
(Sardine stock)

This dashi stock is for miso soup. Iriko of good quality is curved, has blue backs and silvery white bellies.

INGREDIENTS (3 cups)

15~16 iriko / 3 cups water

1. Remove the head and guts and tear.

Remove the bitter head and guts. Tear as far as the tail lengthwise in the form of a pine leaf.

2. Cook over medium heat and remove.

Place iriko and water in a pan and cook over medium heat. When it comes to a boil, reduce the heat and simmer for 3~4 minutes. Turn off the heat and scoop the iriko out.

WATER STOCK OF IRIKO

When you have enough time to prepare the night before, soak the iriko in water overnight. It makes good stock.
Method: Prepare the iriko in the same way as Iriko Dashi. Soak in 3 cups water and add 1 Tbsp sake. Allow to stand overnight.

WATER STOCK OF KOMBU

Used for vegetarian dishes and the fish dishes which are spoiled by the smell of bonito.

INGREDIENTS (3 cups)

2 pieces kombu (6×2"(15×5cm))
3 cups water

Method: Wipe the kombu with a dry cloth to remove dirt and sand. Soak in water for 1 hour and strain through cheesecloth. In summer and for daily use, keep it in the refrigerator overnight.

SHIITAKE MUSHROOM STOCK

This stock is used for vegetarian dishes. If the smell is too strong, combine with kombu stock.

INGREDIENTS (3 cups)

3~4 dried shiitake mushrooms
3 cups water

Method: Wash shiitake quickly in water and soak in measured water. Place a drop lid to prevent from floating. Keep in dark and cold place for half a day.

How to Make Use of the Kombu Used for Dashi

Dry the kombu after making dashi and store in an airtight container. You may cook it to go with o-chazuke (cooked rice with tea) and simple meals.
Ingredients & Method:
① Soak 2 1/2 oz (70 g) dried kombu in ample water for 30 minutes to soften. Cut into 1 1/4"(3 cm) square pieces.
② Place the kombu and water in a pan and add 1/4 tsp vinegar. Simmer over low heat, adding water if necessary, until tender.
③ Add 4 Tbsp sake and 4 Tbsp soy sauce and continue to simmer over low heat until the liquid is almost gone.

MISO SOUPS

Miso-shiru

Miso soup is one of the essential items eaten daily with cooked rice. Since miso has a strong taste and smell, iriko dashi stock (p.109) is used.

TIPS

1. Cook those ingredients that take longer to cook or add flavor in the dashi stock.
2. Once miso is dissolved, never bring to a boil or the flavor will dissipate.
3. Ingredients such as tofu and wakame should be added last and turn off the heat. Serve immediately.

Asparagus and Udo — Spring

The combination of spring vegetables looks attractive. This soup has a plain taste. Shinshu-miso (p. 114) goes well with this soup.

INGREDIENTS

4 green asparagus / 1/4 stalk udo / 2 cups dashi stock / 1 1/2 oz (40 g) miso

PREPARATION

① Trim off and discard the tough ends of the asparagus. Cut the stalks into 1 1/4" (3 cm) lengths.
② Cut the udo in half crosswise. Pare the skin rather thick and cut into thin rectangle pieces.

METHOD

① Bring the dashi stock to a boil and cook the asparagus over medium heat for 4~5 minutes.
② Strain the miso and dissolve in the soup and bring to a boil.
③ Scatter the udo over the soup and turn off the heat. Serve immediately.

Okra and Tofu — Summer

In hot summer, thick miso soup is suitable. Use hatcho miso (p. 114) and make a plain soup.

INGREDIENTS

4 pods okra / 1/3 block kinugoshi-dofu (silken tofu) / 2 cups dashi stock / 1 3/4 oz (50 g) hatcho-miso

PREPARATION

① Rub okra lightly with salt to remove fuzz. Plunge in boiling water and transfer to ice water. Pat dry and cut into round thin slices.
② Cut tofu into 3/8" (1 cm) cubes.

METHOD

① In a pan bring the dashi stock to a boil and dissolve the miso.
② Add the tofu and turn off the heat just before boiling.
③ Ladle the soup in serving bowls and scatter the okra slices over.

Shimeji Mushrooms and Tofu Autumn

Seasonable shimeji mushrooms are one of the best ingredients for autumn miso soup. Use Shinshu-miso (p. 114).

INGREDIENTS

1/2 pack shimeji mushrooms / 1/3 block kinugoshi-dofu (silken tofu) / 2 cups dashi stock / 1 3/4 oz (50 g) miso

PREPARATION

① Break the shimeji into small clumps and wash quickly. Cut off the base ends.
② Cut the tofu into rectangular pieces about 3/8" (1 cm) wide. Cut these pieces into long sticks about 3/8" (1 cm) wide.

METHOD

① In a pan bring the dashi stock to a boil. Add the shimeji and bring to a boil again.
② Strain the miso and dissolve in the soup.
③ Add the tofu and cook. Turn off the heat just before boiling. Serve hot.

Gurnard and Burdock Winter

A luxurious miso soup with gurnard, white fish and burdock.

INGREDIENTS

1 small gurnard / 1 1/2 oz (40 g) burdock / 1/3 stalk naganegi / 3 cups dashi stock / 2 1/8 oz (60 g) miso / 1 tsp sake

PREPARATION

① Scale the fish. Remove the head and innards and wash in running water quickly. Cut into 4 round portions.
② Place in a bamboo colander. Pour boiling water over. Plunge in ice water and remove the dark flesh and remaining scales.
③ Wash the burdock and make shaving cuts (sasagaki, p.12). Soak in vinegared water, then wash in water. Cut the naganegi in round thin slices.

METHOD

① In a pan bring the dashi stock to a boil and cook the fish over medium heat for 3~4 minutes.
② Add the burdock and bring to a boil.
③ Strain the miso and dissolve in the soup. Add the sake to season.
④ Just before boiling, scatter the negi slices over and turn off the heat.

CLEAR SOUPS

Suimono

Clear soups look a little more ceremonious than miso soups. For the dashi, bonito stock and kombu stock are used. The cut of ingredients, the color and attractive serving are important.

TIPS

1. The taste of clear soups depends on the dashi stock. Use ichiban dashi or water stock of kombu.
2. Ingredients such as fish and chicken make the soup cloudy, so prepare them carefully by parboiling or cooking in advance.
3. To make soups clear, use light (not dark) soy sauce.

Vegetable Soup — Spring

Colorful julienne vegetables look attractive. The combined vegetables give this soup a plain but rich taste.

INGREDIENTS

3/4 oz (20 g) carrot / 1 oz (30 g) burdock / 1/4 stalk udo / 1 (8"/20 cm) butterbur / 2 fresh shiitake mushrooms / 10 broad beans / **Broth** <2 cups dashi stock / 1/2 tsp salt / 1 tsp light soy sauce / 1 tsp sake> / Kinome (sansho pepper leaves)

PREPARATION

① Cut the carrot, burdock and udo into julienne pieces. Dip the burdock and udo in vinegared water to remove harshness. Cut off the stems of shiitake and cut into thin slices.
② Parboil the butterbur as shown on page 18. Cut diagonally into thin slices. Parboil broad beans in salted water.

METHOD

① Bring the stock to a boil in a pan. Simmer the burdock, shiitake and carrot over medium heat for 3~4 minutes.
② Add the seasonings to taste. Add the butterbur, udo and peeled broad beans. Turn off the heat. Serve in a bowl and top with kinome.

Sea Bass and Harusame Soup — Summer

Sea bass is in season in the summer. It puts on fat in this season. Use a green yuzu citron rind as garnish.

INGREDIENTS

2 fillets sea bass / Harusame (starch noodles) / 1 myoga-take / **Broth** <2 cups dashi stock / 1 tsp salt / Dash light soy sauce / 1 tsp sake> / Green yuzu citron rind

PREPARATION

① Place the sea bass fillets on a bamboo colander. Sprinkle with salt. Pour first boiling water and then ice water over.
② Soak the harusame in boiling water until transparent and cool in water. Strain and cut into bite-sized lengths.
③ Cut the myoga-take in half lengthwise and then diagonally into thin slices.

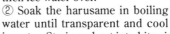

METHOD

① Bring the dashi stock to a boil in a pan and add seasonings.
② Heat the sea bass quickly in the broth and transfer to a serving bowl. Add the harusame and myoga-take and cover with the broth. Top with a citron rind.

Mushrooms and Curdled Egg Soup   Autumn

Pour boiling water over eggs combined with other ingredients and gathers them up with cloth. This is called 'shime-tamago' (curdled eggs). Using seasonal mushrooms make small dumplings.

INGREDIENTS

2 eggs / Dash salt / 1/3 pack shimeji mushrooms / (A) <1 tsp sake / 1/2 tsp light soy sauce> / 1/2 pack kaiware (daikon sprouts) / **Broth** <2 cups dashi stock / 2/3 tsp salt / 1 tsp light soy sauce / 1 tsp sake> / Citron rinds

PREPARATION

① Cut off the base ends of clumps of the shimeji. Parboil quickly and transfer to a colander. Sprinkle with (A) mixture.
② Beat the eggs and season with a dash salt. Add the shimeji ①.
③ Pour the egg mixture over into boiling water. When it floats to the surface, pour into a cloth-lined colander. Roll up in the cloth. Twist both ends of the cloth and form the shape with a bamboo mat. Let stand until cooled.

METHOD

① Bring the dashi stock to a boil in a pan and add seasonings.
② Cut the egg roll into 6 portions and place in serving bowls. Add parboiled kaiware and cover with the broth. Top with twists of the citron rinds (p. 153).

Scallops and Vegetable Soup   Winter

A rich homey soup with scallops and vegetables. Since it is thickened with cornstarch, it does not cool quickly, making it suitable for the cold season.

INGREDIENTS

4 scallops (canned) / 2 taros / 3 1/2 oz (100 g) daikon radish / 1 1/2 oz (40 g) burdock/ carrot / 2 fresh shiitake mushrooms / **Broth** <2 cups dashi stock / 1 canned scallop liquid / 1/2 tsp salt / 1 tsp light soy sauce / 1 tsp sake> / 2/3 Tbsp cornstarch / Mitsuba (honewort)

PREPARATION

① Break scallops into flakes roughly.
② Cut the taros into half-moon slices 1/4" (5 mm) thick. Cut the daikon, carrot and shiitake into icho-giri(p.10). Cut the burdock diagonally into thin slices and soak in vinegared water. Cut the mitsuba into bite-sized pieces.

METHOD

① In the stock and liquid of canned scallops, cook the scallops and vegetables except mitsuba over medium heat.
② Add seasonings when the taros become soft.
③ Add the cornstarch dissolved in 1 1/3 Tbsp water and bring to a boil to thicken the soup. Top with the mitsuba and serve immediately in a bowl.

TIPS FOR SOUPS

How to choose miso

Miso varies greatly in terms of ingredients, saltiness, color, flavor, and texture, depending on the region in which it was made. Generally, Hatcho-miso, which has a sharp, concentrated flavor, and Echigo-miso are used in summer. Sweet white Saikyo-miso is used in winter. Shinshu-miso is used all through the year.

However, try many kinds of miso to decide which ones you like best. You can mix two kinds of miso to enjoy a mild and rich taste.

The point is to mix the two kinds of miso of different textures, and another point is to choose the miso from different regions.

Saikyo-miso (white)　　Shinshu-miso　　Hatcho-miso (red)

Don't boil.

Dissolve miso just before serving to retain its smell and flavor. Once miso is added, never bring the soup to a boil. It will spoil the taste to re-heat it, so set it aside without adding miso for those who will eat later.

Wan-dane, Wan-zuma, Sui-kuchi

Wan-dane　　Wan-zuma　　Sui-Kuchi

Japanese clear soup consists of three items, wan-dane, wan-zuma and sui-kuchi and they are combined according to seasons.

■ Wan-dane
Principal ingredients such as seafood, chicken, eggs, and tofu, which have little fat and contain protein.
■ Wan-zuma
Seasonable vegetables and yuba (dried soybean casein), seaweed and harusame (starch noodles). Choose in combination with wan-dane. If you desire colorful soup, you may add two kinds.
■ Sui-kuchi
Something which adds aroma. Typical seasonable sui-kuchi is shown in the photos. See page 153 for cutting the citron. Other sui-kuchi includes powdered sansho (prickly ash), pepper, chili pepper, shichimi-togarashi (seven-spice pepper) and sesame seeds.

SPRING

Kinome　　Fukinoto

SUMMER

Aojiso　　Myoga　　Ao-yuzu

AUTUMN / WINTER

Yuzu

How to serve clear soups

1　Hold the bowl in the palm and place the wan-dane in the center. Spread a little wan-zuma under those that have bones and shells.

2　Add wan-zuma with the color and balance in mind.

3　Pour hot soup over slowly with care not to break the shape.

4　Top with sui-kuchi and place a lid immediately to retain the aroma.

UNIQUE INGREDIENTS

KIKU-NORI

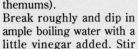

Steamed and dried petals of yellow chrysanthemums. It is also called 'hoshi-giku' (dried chrysanthemums).
Break roughly and dip in ample boiling water with a little vinegar added. Stir with long chopsticks and transfer immediately to a bamboo colander and fan to cool. The aroma and texture suit boiled green vegetables and vinegared food.

★ Broiled Pomfret (p. 42),
  Kiku-nori with Citrus fruit (p.140)

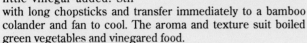

YURI-NE (Lily bulb)

The scaly bulb is a swollen underground stem. The best harvest season is from November to February. It has a little bitter and sweet taste and the texture is similar to potatoes. Each clove is separated and used for Chawan-mushi (steamed egg custard) and Ume-ae (ume dressing). The bulb is also cooked as it is. When dividing the cloves, remove the fine roots, wash in water and separate carefully. Cut into uniform shapes, removing the dirt. Dip in vinegared water and then boil in water with a little vinegar added.

★ Steamed Tilefish and Turnip (p. 62)

GINKGO NUTS

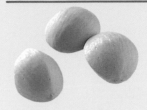

Known for their jade color and bitter taste, these nuts are used for Chawan-mushi (steamed egg custard), Dobin-mushi (matsutake mushrooms cooked in an earthenware teapot) and other dishes for color. To shell the nuts, crush the top with the back of a knife. Dip in boiling water with a dash of salt added and remove the skins by rolling the nuts with the bottom of a draining spoon. Transfer to a bamboo colander to cool.

SUIZENJI-NORI

A kind of algae in fresh water. It is crushed and spread on a tile to dry. It was found growing naturally at Suizenji in Kumamoto prefecture but now it is cultured. When soaked in water, it swells ten times its size. It is used for vinegared dishes and garnishes of sashimi.

BAKUDAIKAI

A kind of nut produced in Sichuan in China. It is as large as the tip of the little finger. When soaked in water, it breaks the skin, swells several times its size and becomes spongy. The taste is plain and it is used for vinegared dishes and garnishes of sashimi.

SEASONAL INGREDIENTS

Make use of ingredients in season

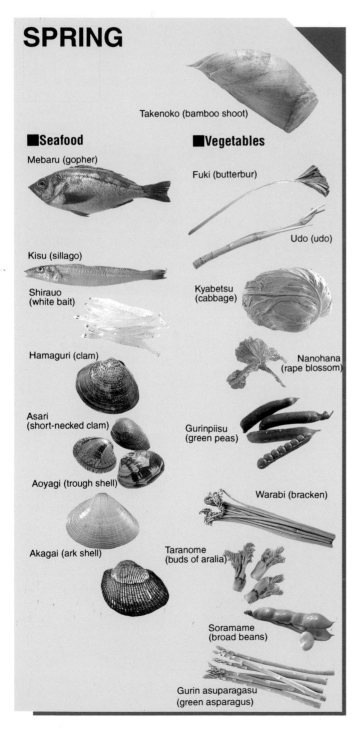

SPRING

Takenoko (bamboo shoot)

■Seafood

Mebaru (gopher)

Kisu (sillago)

Shirauo
(white bait)

Hamaguri (clam)

Asari
(short-necked clam)

Aoyagi (trough shell)

Akagai (ark shell)

■Vegetables

Fuki (butterbur)

Udo (udo)

Kyabetsu
(cabbage)

Nanohana
(rape blossom)

Gurinpiisu
(green peas)

Warabi (bracken)

Taranome
(buds of aralia)

Soramame
(broad beans)

Gurin asuparagasu
(green asparagus)

SUMMER

Kyuri (cucumber)

■Seafood

Aji (horse mackerel)

Kamasu (saury-pike)

Ayu (sweetfish)

Unagi (eel)

Awabi (abalone)

■Vegetables

Tougan (white gourd-melon)

Edamame
(green soybeans)

Shishi-togarashi
(sweet green pepper)

Nasu
(eggplant)

Ingen
(string beans)

Aojiso
(green shiso leaves)

Kabocha (pumpkin)

Tomato (tomato)

Piiman (green pepper)

Okura (okra)

Serori (celery)

Japanese cuisine revolves around seasonal ingredients. In addition to enjoying the changing seasons, each season brings in a rich harvest of crops and offers the freshest ingredients at their peak. Vegetables and fruit are fully ripe and sweet. Seafood puts on fat. They all make daily meals substantial. It is, therefore, important to remember each seasonal material and use it in your menu.

AUTUMN

Matsutake
(matsutake mushroom)

■Seafood

Sanma (saury)

Saba (mackerel)

Sake (salmon)

Wakasagi (pond smelt)

Iwashi (sardine)

■Vegetables

Shimeji
(shimeji mushroom)

Enokidake
(enoki mushroom)

Shiitake (shiitake mushroom)

Maitake
(maitake mushroom)

Shungiku (edible
leafy chrysanthemum)

Renkon (lotus root)

Gobo (burdock)

Satoimo (taro)

Satsumaimo (sweet potato)

Kuri (chestnut)

Ginnan (ginkgo nut)

WINTER

Horenso (spinach)

■Seafood
Buri (yellowtail)

Managatsuo (pomfret)

Karei (flatfish)

Kinmedai
(alfonsino)

Tara (cod)

Sawara (Spanish mackerel)

Hobo (gurnard)

Amadai (bream)

Kaki (oyster)

■Vegetables

Komatsuna (a kind of
Chinese cabbage)

Daikon
(daikon radish)

Kabu (turnip)

Hakusai
(Chinese cabbage)

Naganegi
(Japanese bunching onion)

Seri (Japanese parsley)

Yurine (lily bulb)

Kuwai (arrowhead)

Hotategai (scallop)

SPRING MENUS

The soft sunshine takes the icy chill off the waters. Hills and fields are ablaze with flowering plants. Everything looks bright. Bring this brilliant atmosphere to your table. For seasonal food from the land there are bamboo shoots, butterbur and edible wild plants and for the delicacies from the sea there are clams and short-neck clams.

The dishes should be lightly seasoned and vinegared food should have a sour taste.

Colorful
Spring Dishes

Tosa-ni of Bamboo Shoot and Butterbur
Rape Blossoms and Udo in Karashi-zu
Grilled Scabbard Fish
Clear Bamboo Shoot Soup
Rape-blossom Rice

This menu makes use of typical spring vegetables. Tosa-ni is a dish cooked in a base of soy sauce flavored with bonito flakes. For karashi-zu, see page 69. The rice is covered with scrambled eggs and powdered green tea to look like rape blossoms.

TOSA-NI OF BAMBOO SHOOT AND BUTTERBUR
Takenoko to fuki no tosa-ni

INGREDIENTS

2 small (21 oz / 600 g) bamboo shoots	**Simmering stock**
A handful of rice bran	3/4 cup dashi stock
1 red chili pepper	2 Tbsp sake
7 oz (200 g) butterbur	1 1/2 Tbsp sugar
1 cup bonito flakes	1 Tbsp mirin
Kinome (young leaves of prickly ash)	2 Tbsp soy sauce

Method

① Boil bamboo shoots as shown below. Scrape remaining skins off with the end of a chopstick corner. Cut the top part into quarter and the lower part into 3/8" (1 cm) slices.

② Cut the butterbur into 8" (20 cm) lengths. Sprinkle with salt and roll back and forth on a cutting board. Cook in boiling water and transfer to ice water. Remove skins and strings and cut into 1 1/4" (3 cm) lengths (p. 18).

③ Place bonito flakes in a pan and toast over low heat until crisp. Transfer to a flat container to cool and rub roughly.

④ Place bamboo shoots and dashi stock in a pan over high heat. When it comes to a boil, reduce the heat to medium. Add seasonings and continue simmering.

⑤ When the liquid is reduced to 1/3, add the butterbur and cook until the liquid is almost gone. Transfer to a flat container to cool and sprinkle with bonito flakes. Serve in a bowl and garnish with kinome.

When the dashi stock comes to a boil, add the seasonings one by one.

Cut the top part into bite-sized pieces.

When the bamboo shoots are well seasoned, add the butterbur.

Cool and evaporate the excess water and sprinkle with bonito flakes.

RAPE BLOSSOMS AND UDO IN KARASHI-ZU
Nanohana to udo no karashi-zu

INGREDIENTS

1/2 bunch rape blossoms	**Karashi-zu**
1/3 udo	1 tsp prepared mustard
	1 Tbsp vinegar
	1/3 tsp sugar
	1 Tbsp light soy sauce
	1 Tbsp dashi stock

Method

① Wash the rape blossoms well under running water in a bowl. Cut off the hard parts about 3/4" (2 cm) from the roots.

② Add a dash of salt to ample boiling water. Divide the rape blossoms into two groups of several stalks, and parboil one group at a time until they turn to a bright color. Transfer to ice water to cool. Align in water and squeeze water out. Cut into bite-sized pieces.

③ Cut the udo into 1 1/4" (3 cm) lengths. Pare the thick skin and cut into sticks. Dip in vinegared water to remove harshness and wash quickly in water.

④ Just before serving, combine the ingredients of karashi-zu. Dress the chilled rape blossoms and udo with the karashi-zu and serve colorfully.

How to Boil Bamboo Shoots

1. Cut the top part off diagonally. Make a cut into the bamboo shoot, shallow at the base and gradually deeper out to the tip.

2. Place rice bran and chili pepper in ample water and bring to a boil. Place a drop-lid and boil 40 minutes to one hour, taking care not to let it boil over. The rice bran adds sweetness and the chili pepper removes harshness.

3. If a bamboo skewer easily passes through the thick part, it is done.

4. Set stand to cool covered with the drop-lid. Never take out while hot or the harshness will remain.

5. Wash in water and pare the skin along the cut. Remove the remaining skin with the end of a chopstick.

GRILLED SCABBARD FISH
Tachiuo no kinome-yaki

INGREDIENTS

4 fillets scabbard fish
Dipping sauce
{ 3 Tbsp sake
{ 3 Tbsp mirin
{ 1/2 cup soy sauce

20 kinome
(young leaves of prickly ash)
Grated daikon radish
Grated ginger

Method

① Cut off the dorsal fin of scabbard fish. Make diagonal scores on both sides so as to be well seasoned.
② Combine the ingredients of dipping sauce in a flat container and place the fish on top. Let stand for 1~ 2 hours, occasionally turning over.
③ Insert two metal skewers into two fillets in a fan shape. Grill the serving side first some distance above medium heat until the skewers easily turn around.
④ Coat with dipping sauce and dry over the heat. Repeat this two or three times and pull out the skewers while hot.
⑤ Set aside 4 leaves of kinome for garnishes and cut the other kinome into fine pieces. Place the fish on a plate. Scatter kinome pieces over and garnish with the leaves. Serve with grated daikon radish and ginger in front.

The dorsal fin is hard and offends the eye, so cut it off.	Soak in the dipping sauce and occasionally turn over.

CLEAR BAMBOO SHOOT SOUP
Wakatake-wan

INGREDIENTS

Himekawa (soft inner layers)
   of 2 bamboo shoots
Dry wakame
2 kinome

Broth
{ 2 cups dashi stock
{ 2/3 tsp salt
{ 1 tsp light soy sauce
{ Sake

Typical spring clear soup with soft inner layers of bamboo shoots and wakame. Kinome is usually used in this soup.

Method

① Soak the wakame in ample water for 5 minutes. Remove the stems and cut into 3/4" (2 cm) lengths. Place in a strainer and dip in boiling water quickly and transfer to ice water to bring out the color.
② Cut soft inner layers of bamboo shoots into julienne pieces.
③ Bring the dashi stock to a boil and add the seasonings. Add the bamboo shoots and wakame and heat quickly. Serve in a bowl garnished with kinome.

Note

The soft inner layers of bamboo shoots may also be dressed with ume flesh and sea urchin or used in Japanese-style salad.

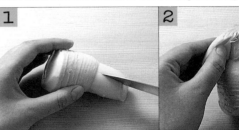

Make a cut slit in the soft part of boiled bamboo shoots and take off the soft layers.	Open the cut and peel the soft part.

DAILY MENUS

In organizing your daily menus, you should make good use of fresh ingredients in season, taking care to have variety. Take care not to use the same kinds of ingredients and similar seasonings. The basic menu consists of cooked rice and a bowl of soup plus several side dishes. For example, a bowl of soup and three kinds of dishes (ichi-juu san-sai), which consist of mukouzuke, nimono and yakimono, are a basic simple meal served to guests before the formal tea ceremony (kaiseki-ryori). The formal soup is a miso soup. A steamed egg custard and dobin-mushi (steamed food in a tea pot) can also be substituted. Mukouzuke is sashimi (sliced raw fish), vinegared dish or a Japanese-style salad. Yakimono is a grilled dish, usually fish fillets, but sweetfish is not cut. Meat and deep-fried dishes can also be substituted. Nimono is a simmered dish and it is the main dish which has seasonal flavor. A small quantity of cooked rice is usually served.

Daily menus are not formal, so rice, a bowl of soup or a salad plus either nimono or yakimono (ichi-juu ni-sai) are enough. In the case of one-pot dishes with various ingredients, add only a Japanese salad. What is important is not how many dishes are served, but the care to serve cold food cold and hot food hot. Take notes of your daily menus and do not forget to serve different kinds of food every day.

ENJOY THE SAVOR OF SPRING

This menu is a combination of delicious food from land and sea. Since beef is included, it is a nutritionally balanced diet. Cabbages are available all the year round. Those in spring are especially soft and sweet, so the leaves have been seasoned with salt and rubbed. Prepare the menu according to the order given in these pages.

CABBAGE AND RADISHES SQUEEZED WITH SALT
Kyabetsu to radisshu no shio-momi

INGREDIENTS

6 leaves (18 oz / 500 g) cabbage
5 radishes

2 myoga (Japanese ginger)
2 tsp salt

Method
① Remove the core of the cabbage and cut into 4 lengthwise. Pile the leaves and cut into pieces about 3/4" (2 cm) wide. Cut the radishes into thin slices.
② Cut the myoga in half lengthwise, and then cut into pieces crosswise. Place in a strainer and dip in boiling water. Transfer to ice water and drain.
③ In a large bowl, place the vegetables and sprinkle with salt. Give a gentle rub at first, then a stronger rub gradually until water comes out and they become tender.
④ Squeeze water out tightly, place in a container and chill in the refrigerator until served.

SIMMERED ZENMAI
Zenmai no tosa-ni

INGREDIENTS

2 1/2 oz (70 g) dried zenmai (royal fern)
2 aburage (deep-fried tofu)
1 Tbsp vegetable oil
Toasted white sesame seeds

Simmering stock
1/2 cup dashi stock
2 Tbsp sake
3 Tbsp sugar
2 Tbsp mirin
2 1/2 ~3 Tbsp soy sauce

Method
① See page 35 for boiling the zenmai. Cut the hard tips off and cut into 1 1/4" (3 cm) lengths.
② Arrange the aburage in a bamboo colander and pour boiling water over to remove the excess oil. Cut in half lengthwise and then into thin strips crosswise about 1/4" (5 mm) wide.
③ Heat the oil in a pan and stir-fry the zenmai quickly over high heat. Add the aburage strips and continue to stir-fry together.
④ Add all the ingredients of the simmering stock and cook over medium heat, occasionally stirring, until the liquid is almost gone. Transfer to a flat container to cool. Sprinkle with sesame seeds and serve.

Stir-fry the zenmai until it becomes oily and rich.

BEEF, BROAD BEANS AND UDO

Gyuniku to soramame, udo no nimono

INGREDIENTS

7 oz (200 g) thin slices beef	**Simmering stock**
18 oz (500 g) broad beans in the pod	2 cups dashi stock
1/2 udo	2 Tbsp sake
Kinome (young leaves of prickly ash)	2 Tbsp mirin
	3 Tbsp light soy sauce

Method

① Cut the beef crosswise against the grain into bite-sized pieces.

② Shell the broad beans and make small cuts at the bottom of each bean so it will peel easily. Boil in water with a dash of salt added for about 2 minutes. Transfer to a bamboo colander to cool. Remove the skins. (See page 69)

③ Cut the udo into 1 1/2" (4 cm) lengths and peel the thick skin. Cut into bars. Dip in vinegared water to remove harshness. Wash quickly in water.

④ Bring the dashi stock to a boil and add the seasonings. Add the beef, breaking up. Cook over medium heat until the color changes and skim scum off.

⑤ Gather the beef at the edge of the pan and add the broad beans, continuing to cook. Add the udo last and cook until just done.

⑥ Arrange the whole in a bowl and cover with the liquid. Garnish with kinome.

PAN-FRIED CLAMS

Hamaguri no furaipan-yaki

INGREDIENTS

12 clams	1 Tbsp soy sauce
1 Tbsp sake	Powdered pepper

Method

① Use fresh clams which give a clear sound when hit together. Scrub them with a brush.

② Place side by side in a frying pan over high heat. Pour 1/4 cup water over and cover with a lid. Shake the frying pan until the clams open.

③ Take out the flesh. Sprinkle with sake and soy sauce and let stand for 3 ~ 4 minutes.

④ Bring the liquid of ③ to a boil and add the clams. Cook for a short time until they swell and are well seasoned.

⑤ Spear with a skewer while hot. Serve with powdered pepper on the side.

Pour water over and cover the pan with a lid to steam the clams until open.	Dip the flesh of clams in the sake and soy sauce mixture in advance.

SPRING DISHES IN SMALL BOWLS

POUNDED BRACKEN

Warabi-tororo

A simple dish of pounded, sticky bracken. Ginger flavor goes well with the aroma of bracken.

Ingredients: 3 1/2 oz (100g) boiled bracken / Grated ginger / **Vinegar mixture** <1/2 Tbsp vinegar / 1 Tbsp soy sauce / 1 Tbsp dashi stock>

Method
① Pound the bracken lightly on a cutting board with a wooden pestle until sticky. Cut into 1 1/4" (3 cm) lengths.
② Serve in a bowl topped with grated ginger. Pour the vinegar mixture in from the side.

CABBAGE SIMMERED WITH VINEGAR

Kyabetsu no su-ni

Enjoy a slightly sour tasting soft spring cabbage. Eat while hot or chilled as desired.

Ingredients: 5 leaves (18 oz / 500 g) cabbage / 1 oz (30 g) carrot / **Simmering stock** <1/2 cup dashi stock / 1 Tbsp sake / 1 1/2 Tbsp sugar / 1/2 Tbsp mirin / 1 1/2 light soy sauce> / 1 1/2 Tbsp vinegar

Method
① Discard stems of cabbage and cut into bite-sized pieces. Cut the carrot into julienne strips.
② Bring the simmering stock to a boil in a pan and add the cabbage, carrot and vinegar. Simmer over high heat until tender. Turn upside down and continue cooking until the whole becomes soft.

GREEN PEAS THICKENED WITH KUZU

Grinpiisu no yoshino-ni

Kuzu, thickening agent, comes from Yoshino in Nara Prefecture; hence the name 'Yoshino-ni.' Cornstarch is usually substituted at home.

Ingredients: 18 oz (500 g) green peas with pods (7 oz / 200 g shelled) / 1/2 kamaboko (steamed fish-paste cake) / 1 oz (30 g) carrot / **Simmering stock** <1 1/2 cup dashi stock / 3 Tbsp mirin / 1 1/2 Tbsp light soy sauce / Dash salt> / 1/2 Tbsp cornstarch

Method
① Shell green peas and parboil in salted water for 5 minutes until the color changes to fresh green. Transfer to a bamboo colander.
② Dice the kamaboko and carrot to the size of the green peas.
③ Bring the simmering stock to a boil in a pan and add the carrot. Simmer over low heat for 4~5 minutes.
④ Add the kamaboko and green peas and cook briefly. Dissolve the cornstarch in 1 Tbsp water and pour over to thicken the liquid.

124

MITSUBA AND CHICKEN WITH WASABI VINEGAR

Ne-mitsuba to sasami no wasabi-zu

A plain, unsweetened vinegared dish of mitsuba (honewort).

Ingredients: 1/2 bunch honewort / 2 fillets chicken breast / **(A)** <salt / Pepper / 3 Tbsp sake> / **Vinegar mixture** <1 Tbsp vinegar / 1 Tbsp light soy sauce / 1 Tbsp dashi stock> / Grated wasabi (horse radish) / Benitade (red smartweed)

Method
① Trim off the root of honewort and wash well. Cut in half and parboil in salted water. Dip in ice water and squeeze the water out. Cut into 1 1/4" (3 cm) lengths.
② Remove the skin and sinews from the chicken. Cut open as shown on page 128. Place in a pan and sprinkle (A) over. Cover with an aluminum drop-lid and simmer over low heat until the liquid is gone. Set aside until cool and tear into fine strips.
③ Chill the honewort and chicken and arrange in a bowl. Pour the vinegar mixture over and top with benitade. Serve with the grated wasabi.

TARANOME WITH SESAME DRESSING

Taranome no goma-ae

The tempura of taranome (buds of aralia) is very popular, but the goma-ae is also good. Smaller and younger buds are soft and delicious.

Ingredients: 20 small taranome / 1/2 tsp light soy sauce / **Sesame dressing** <4 Tbsp toasted white sesame seeds / 1/2 Tbsp sake / 2/3 Tbsp soy sauce> / Umezu-shoga (sweet-vinegared ginger)

Method
① Cut off the end of taranome and peel the sheath. Make a cut on a large one and tear in half lengthwise.
② Parboil in slightly salted water for 30 seconds to improve color. Dip in ice water. Drain and sprinkle with soy sauce.
③ Grind sesame seeds in a mortar and mix with the seasonings. Coat the taranome with the sesame dressing well.
④ Serve in a bowl and garnish with umezu-shoga cut in the shape of cherry petals.

KIMPIRA OF UDO SKIN

Udo no kawa no kimpira

The skin of udo has a delicate aroma. Cook quickly to make it crispy.

Ingredients: 5 1/4 oz (150 g) udo skin (1/2~1 stalk) / 1 red chili pepper / 1 Tbsp sesame oil / 1 Tbsp light soy sauce / Dash salt / Poppy seeds

Method
① Scrape the udo skin with the tip of a knife to remove the downy hair. Cut into julienne strips. Soak in slightly vinegared water to remove harshness until the water changes to brown. Rinse quickly in water and drain.
② Soak the red chili pepper in water to soften. Remove seeds and cut into round thin slices from the end.
③ Heat the sesame oil in a pan and stir-fry the udo skin and red chili pepper quickly over high heat.
④ Pour the seasonings over and transfer to a flat container to cool. Serve in a bowl and sprinkle the poppy seeds over.

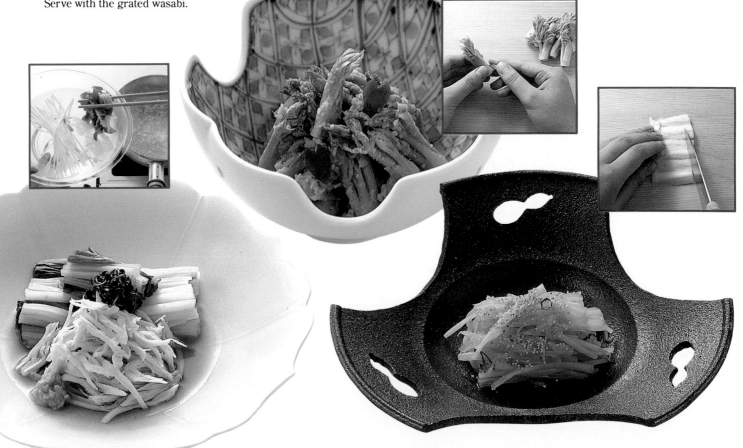

SUMMER MENUS

The heat of summer dulls our appetite and we tend to desire cold and plain dishes.

If we eat only cold meals, the summer heat will wear us down, so it is necessary to have warm dishes and deep-fried food as a balance.

Summer vegetables such as cucumbers and eggplants are in season and horse mackerel and sea bass are just ready to eat. Vinegared dishes will activate the stomach and stimulate the appetite.

A Cool Breeze To The Table

Dressed Greens
Deep-fried Chicken with Aojiso
Miso-soup of Corbiculae
Ume Rice
Wax Gourd and Shrimp

This menu consists of crisp summer vegetables quickly plunged into boiling water, wax gourd cooked until soft and chilled, and deep-fried hot chicken with aromatic aojiso.

Rich miso-soup of corbiculae and plain ume rice are accompanied. This summer menu bring coolness to the table and is refreshing to the eye.

DRESSED GREENS
Seirei-ae

INGREDIENTS

1/2 cucumber	**Vinegar mixture**
2 myoga (Japanese ginger)	1 Tbsp vinegar
5 sweet pepper	1/2 Tbsp sugar
Green soybeans in pods	1/2 tsp light soy sauce
Dried wakame	Dash salt
	1 1/2 Tbsp dashi stock

Method

① Sprinkle salt over the cucumber and rub on a cutting board. Plunge into boiling water and then in ice water. Cut into thin round slices and dip in salted water until soft. Wring the water out.

② Rinse the myoga in water. Cut in half lengthwise thinly. Plunge into boiling water and then ice water. Wring the water out.

③ Remove seeds of the pepper and cut into julienne strips. Boil quickly in salted water. Boil the soybeans in salted water, shell and remove thin skins. Mince roughly.

④ Soak the wakame in water for 5 minutes. Remove the stems and cut into 3/8" (1 cm) lengths. Plunge into boiling water and then ice water to bring out the color.

⑤ Chill the vegetables and wakame in the refrigerator. Dress with the vinegar mixture just before serving.

Use a strainer for parboiling and cooling each set of vegetables.

MISO SOUP OF CORBICULAE
Shijimi no miso-shiru

INGREDIENTS

7 oz (200 g) corbiculae	2 cups dashi stock
Powdered pepper	1 3/4 oz (50 g) hatcho-miso (p. 85)

Method

① Wash the corbiculae under running water, rubbing together. Transfer to a bamboo colander to drain. (See page 156)

② Bring the dashi stock to a boil and add the corbiculae. Bring again to a boil over medium heat, skimming any scum off.

③ Turn off the heat when the shells open. Scoop up with a strainer and strain through cloth to remove remaining sand.

④ Transfer to a clean pan. When it comes to a boil, add the miso and dissolve. When it comes to a boil again, turn off the heat.

⑤ Place the corbiculae in a bowl and cover with the liquid. Sprinkle with powdered pepper to serve.

UME RICE
Tataki ume-gohan

INGREDIENTS

2 cups cooked rice	1 pickled ume

Method

Mince the ume flesh and mix with hot cooked rice.

DEEP-FRIED CHICKEN WITH AOJISO
Sasami no aojiso-age

INGREDIENTS

3 small chicken breasts	Cornstarch
Dash salt	Egg white
1 tsp sake	1/2 cup tentsuyu (see p. 50)
20 aojiso (green shiso leaves)	Oil for deep-frying

Method

① See page 50 for preparing the tentsuyu.

② Remove thin skins and strings of chicken breasts. Cut open to right and left. Cut diagonally into thin strips and season with the sake and salt.

③ Rinse the aojiso in water quickly and drain. Cut in half lengthwise. Roll the whole up and cut into julienne strips from the end.

④ Dredge the chicken with cornstarch, dip into beaten egg white and mix with the aojiso strips.

⑤ Preheat the oil to 340°F (170°C). Using chopsticks, drop a bite-sized in and deep-fry slowly, taking care not to burn. Drain completely and serve while hot with the tentsuyu.

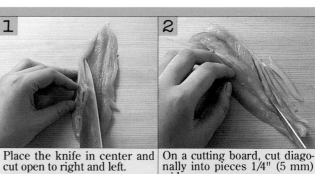

1 Place the knife in center and cut open to right and left.

2 On a cutting board, cut diagonally into pieces 1/4" (5 mm) wide.

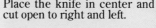

3 Dredge with cornstarch, dip in egg white and then mix with aojiso.

4 Pick up a bite-sized piece of chicken with chopsticks and deep-fry until crisp.

WAX GOURD AND SHRIMP
Togan to ebi no hiyashi-bachi

INGREDIENTS

18 oz (500 g) wax gourd
4 shrimp
1 1/2 Tbsp cornstarch
Green yuzu citron

Simmering stock
3 cups dashi stock
1 Tbsp sake
1/2 Tbsp salt
1/2 Tbsp light soy sauce

Method

① Remove the seeds and inside of the wax gourd. Cut into 1 1/2" (4 cm) cubes and pare. Cut the corners slightly off of each cube so as to keep the shape while cooking.

② Cook for about 20 minutes in boiling water with a dash of salt added until a skewer pierces easily. Transfer to water to cool.

③ Devein shrimp with a bamboo skewer. Boil quickly in salted water until the color changes to bright red. Transfer to a bamboo colander to cool. Remove the head, tail, shell and chop roughly.

④ Bring the dashi stock to a boil and add the wax gourd. When it comes to a boil again, add all the seasonings. Cover with a paper lid, and simmer over lower heat for about 12~13 minutes to season well.

⑤ Scatter shrimp over. Add the cornstarch dissolved in the same amount of water to thicken. Immediately cool by placing the pan in ice water. When cooled, chill in the refrigerator.

⑥ Place in a bowl and cover with the liquid. Scatter grated green yuzu citron over.

Note

Use a fully ripened wax gourd, which has white powder on the surface. Unripe ones have downy hair.

1

2

Scoop out the seeds and inside of wax gourd.

Cut into pieces a little larger than bite-size. Cut off the remaining inside.

3

4

Boil well until a bamboo skewer pierces easily.

Since the flesh is soft, use a paper drop-lid.

5

6

Pour the prepared cornstarch over to thicken.

Cool immediately by placing the pan in ice water.

TABLE SETTINGS

The basic rule is to place a bowl of steamed rice on your left aligned with the soup on your right. The chopsticks are placed in the front with the tips pointing to your left.

On a formal occasion, the rice and soup are served first and then sashimi and foods dressed with sauce. In the course of the meal, a simmered dish and a grilled or fried dish are served. At home, however, all the dishes should be placed at one time so that you can enjoy conversation during the meal without repeatedly rising from your seat.

Japanese cuisine makes great use of seasonal ingredients and the daily table conveys the sense of each season. In summer, use cool glassware and wet unglazed ware to suggest coolness. In winter, warm chinaware brings out the delicacies of cooking. For a change, you may use a server of lacquerware or Japanese paper for a luncheon mat. A flower in season will substitute for a chopstick rest. Arrange wild flowers in a simple vase. All these will go a long way to creating a fancy atmosphere. A little effort will make your daily meal more enjoyable.

THE EVENING MEAL IN SUMMER

The savory smell of grilled eggplants, a light and dry texture of simmered squash those are pleasures of the table in summer. The sashimi of sea bass, patted with cornstarch and dipped in boiling water, has a plain taste. Myoga adds a unique flavor to the miso soup of string beans and aburage. The rice is sprinkled with powdered tea. Satisfy your appetite with this colorful and refreshing menu.

GRILLED EGGPLANTS
Yaki-nasu

INGREDIENTS

3 eggplants
1 ginger

Shaved bonito

Method
① Make a cut around the calyx about 3/4" (2 cm) below the top. Remove the points.
② Heat a grill and place the eggplants on top. Grill the whole, rolling occasionally over high heat.
③ Check doneness by picking with chopsticks. If soft, dip in ice water and peel quickly in the water. Cut off the calyx and cut into bite-sized pieces.
④ Serve in a plate with garnishes of grated ginger and shaved bonito.

Grill until the skin scorches crisply.

Peel the skin immediately while hot.

SWEETENED SQUASH
Kabocha no ama-ni

INGREDIENTS

10 1/2 oz (300 g) squash
Green soybeans

3 Tbsp sugar
1/2 Tbsp light soy sauce

Method
① Remove the seeds and inside from the squash. Cut into cubes, 1 1/4 × 1 1/2" (3 × 4 cm). Scrape the skin partly and dip in water to remove harshness. Wash quickly, changing the water 2 or 3 times. Drain in a bamboo colander.
② Arrange the squash in a pan with the skin side down. Fill with water, covering barely the surface (about 1 1/2 cups). Add the seasonings and cook over high heat.
③ When it comes to a boil, skim off any scum. Cover with a aluminum drop-lid. Continue simmering over medium heat until the liquid is almost gone.
④ Transfer to a flat container to cool. Serve in a bowl with green soybeans scattered over.

Cut off of the four sides to prevent from breaking up .

SEA BASS
Suzuki no kuzu-uchi

INGREDIENTS

5 1/4 oz (150 g) sea bass
Cornstarch
1/2 cucumber
2 aojiso (green shiso leaves)

Dried wakame seaweed
Benitade (red smartweed)
Wasabi horseradish
1 pickled ume

Method
① Sprinkle a dash of salt over the cucumber and rub on a cutting board. Cut from the end into thin slices and dip in salted water. When it becomes soft, squeeze the excess water out. Soak the wakame in water for about 5 minutes. Remove the stems and cut into bite-sized pieces. Parboil and then transfer to cold water to bring out the color. Drain.
② Cut fresh sea bass into thin slices using a slightly slanted knife (sogi-giri, p. 10). Pat the slices with a gauze pack of cornstarch and drop in boiling water one by one.
③ When the cornstarch turns transparent (it takes about 10 seconds), transfer to ice water and then drain on a wet cloth spread in a bamboo colander.
④ Stand aojiso between crushed ice in a bowl and place the fish in front. Garnish with the cucumber, wakame, benitade and add the wasabi and chopped flesh of ume.

Put powder in a gauze pack to prevent from powdering too much.

When the cornstarch turns transparent, dip the fish in ice water.

MISO SOUP OF STRING BEANS AND MYOGA
Ingen to myoga no miso-shiru

INGREDIENTS

6 string beans
1/2 pices aburage
(deep-fried tofu)

2 1/2 cups dashi stock
1 3/4 oz (50 g) miso
1 myoga (Japanese ginger)

Method
① Remove strings from the string beans and cut into 1 1/4" (3 cm) lengths. Wash the myoga in water and cut from the end into round slices. Pour boiling water over the aburage to remove the excess oil. Cut in half lengthwise and then crosswise into strips about 1/4" (5 mm) wide.
② Place the dashi stock, string beans and aburage in a pan and cook over medium heat for 5~6 minutes.
③ Dissolve the miso. When it comes to a boil, add the myoga and turn off the heat immediately. Serve in a bowl while hot.

To eat with alcoholic beverages
SUMMER DISHES IN SMALL BOWLS

DRESSED SUMMER VEGETABLE CUBES
Natsu-yasai no kokaku-ae

A salad-style dressed dish. Since oil is used, the vegetables do not become watery if kept for a long time.

Ingredients: 1/2 cucumber / 1/3 stalk celery / 1/4 tomato / 1/2 eggplant / carrot / 2/3 Tbsp sesame oil / 1 Tbsp light soy sauce

Method
① Rub the cucumber with salt on a cutting board and rinse in water. Quarter lengthwise and remove the seeds. Cut into 3/8" (8 mm) cubes.
② Remove tough fibers from the celery. Peel the tomato and deseed. Cut all into the cubes of the same size. Soak the eggplant cubes in water and drain completely.
③ Chill the vegetables. Combine with the sesame oil and soy sauce just before serving.

BONITO FLAKES IN GREEN PEPPERS
Piiman okaka

The smell of scorched soy sauce stimulates your appetite. The important point is to stuff bonito flakes lightly.

Ingredients: 3 green peppers / 3/16 oz (5 g) fine bonito flakes / 1/2 Tbsp sake / 2/3 Tbsp soy sauce

Method
① Wash the peppers quickly. Trim off each stem and remove the seeds.
② Sprinkle sake and soy sauce over the bonito flakes and mix quickly. Stuff lightly in each pepper evenly.
③ Place on a heated grill and grill, rolling over high heat quickly until slightly scorched.
④ Cut into bite-sized pieces and serve on a plate.

VINEGARED PICKLING MELON
Shiro-uri no sunomono

A pale green melon cucumber is refreshing to the eye. If dipped in boiling water, it is edible with the skin.

Ingredients: 7oz (200 g) pickling melon / **Vinegar mixture** <1 1/2 Tbsp vinegar / 2/3 Tbsp sugar / 1/3 tsp light soy sauce / 1 1/2 dashi stock> / Toasted black sesame seeds / Murame (buds of red shiso)

Method
① Wash the pickling melon in water and rub ample salt with hands.
② Thrust with a fork and dip in boiling water quickly and then in ice water. Cut in half lengthwise and remove the seeds. Cut diagonally into thin slices.
③ Soak in salted water (as salty as brine) for 15 minutes until tender. Squeeze the water out firmly.
④ Mix with the vinegar mixture and chill until serving. Serve in a bowl topped with murame. Sprinkle with the sesame seeds.

CHILLED TOFU

Kawari hiya-yakko

A variation of chilled tofu. Enjoy the unexpected combination with hot pollack roe and shallot.

Ingredients: 2/3 block kinugoshi-dofu (silken tofu) / 1/2 mentaiko (pollack roe salted and flavored with chili pepper) / 2 tsp sake / 3 shallots / 1 Tbsp sesame seed oil

Method
① Cut the tofu into 1 1/2" (4 cm) cubes. Drain on dishcloth. Set aside in a bowl and chill.
② Chop the mentaiko roughly and sprinkle sake over. Remove fine roots of shallot and cut into round thin slices.
③ Heat the sesame oil in a frying pan and stir-fry the mentaiko until the surface color changes.
④ Add the shallot and mix together. Place on the top of the tofu.

MOUNTAIN YAM WITH UME FLESH

Tataki yamaimo no bainiku-ae

Use a thick and fully ripe mountain yam. It is crispy and ume flesh gives a refreshing taste.

Ingredients: 5 1/4 oz (150 g) mountain yam / 1 pickled ume / Green soy beans

Method
① Wash the mountain yam. Pare the thick skin.
② Wet dishcloth and wring tightly. Wrap the yam in the wet dishcloth and pound with a wooden pestle to crush roughly.
③ Remove the seed of a pickled ume and chop the flesh.
④ Arrange the yam in a bowl. Scatter the ume flesh and green soybeans over. If you desire, add soy sauce and mix lightly before eating.

STRING BEANS WRAPPED IN SHISO

Ingen no maki nanban

Wrap string beans in shiso leaves and season with shichimi-togarashi (seven-spice pepper) and hatcho-miso. Fried in sesame seed oil, this dish will surely stimulate your appetite.

Ingredients: 15 string beans / 10 aojiso (green shiso leaves) / **Nanban-miso** <1 Tbsp hatcho-miso (p. 85) / 1 1/2 Tbsp sugar / 1/2 tsp shichimi-togarashi (seven-spice pepper)> / 1 Tbsp sesame oil

Method
① String the beans and parboil in salted water. Transfer to a bamboo colander and fan to cool. Cut in half. Wash the shiso leaves and drain completely.
② Make nanban-miso by combining the miso, sugar and shichimi in a small bowl.
③ Place 3 string beans on the back of a shiso leaf. Put a small quantity of miso (as much as the tip of your little finger). Roll up.
④ Heat the sesame oil in a frying pan and then remove it from heat. Place ③ with the rolled-up end down. Return the pan to the heat and fry over medium heat.
⑤ Turn upside down when aromatic. When all rolls are turned over, turn off the heat and serve on a plate.

AUTUMN MENUS

As autumn advances, the leaves turn red and chestnuts and mushrooms ripen. Branches of persimmons and grapes become heavy with fruit.

Blue fish like saury, mackerel and sardine are in season and delicious.

Let's give thanks for the harvest of autumn and make substantial and rich dishes. Vinegared dishes should be less sour, so season them lightly.

Appreciate
The Harvest Season

Matsutake Mushrooms in a Teapot
Shungiku with Walnut Dressing
Mountain Yam Rolled in Beef
Chestnut Rice

Matsutake mushrooms, chestnuts and chrysanthemums —autumnal food is now ready to eat.
Prepare dobin-mushi (matsutake mushrooms in a teapot) in place of soup. Eat when matsutake expand and become soft. Cook rice with chestnuts, and coat shungiku (edible leafy chrysanthemum) with walnut dressing. Season crisp mountain yam rolled in beef with wine and soy sauce.

MATSUTAKE MUSHROOMS IN A TEAPOT
Matsutake no dobin-mushi

INGREDIENTS

{ 2 matsutake mushrooms
{ 1/2 Tbsp sake

{ 1 chicken breast
{ Dash light soy sauce
{ 1 tsp sake

2 shrimp
4 slices kamaboko
   (steamed fish-paste cake)
6 ginkgo nuts

Mitsuba (honewort)

Broth
{ 1 1/2 cups dashi stock
{ 2/3 tsp salt
{ 1 tsp light soy sauce
{ 1/2 Tbsp sake
Sake
Sudachi (citrus fruit)

Method

① Select thick and elastic matsutake. Wipe gently, pressing with soft, wet cloth with care not to remove surface skin.
② Slice off the hard stem end of the matsutake diagonally as if sharpening a pencil. Cut the stems into 4~6 portions lengthwise and sprinkle with 1/2 Tbsp sake.
③ Remove the skin and sinews from the chicken breast. Slice diagonally and season with soy sauce and sake. Let stand for about 5 minutes.
④ Devein the shrimp. Cook in lightly salted boiling water until the color changes. Transfer to a colander to cool. Remove the head and shell.
⑤ Shell the ginkgo nuts. Boil in salted water and remove the thin skin (see p. 115). Tie the mitsuba as shown on page 152.
⑥ Bring the dashi stock to a boil and add the seasonings.
⑦ Place the kamaboko in individual earthenware teapots. Divide other ingredients in half and add to each pot. Cover with hot broth.
⑧ Place the teapots on a grill over heat. When it comes to a boil, add 1/2 Tbsp sake and garnish with the mitsuba. Turn off the heat and cover with a lid. Serve on a saucer with the sudachi in a sake cup.

1

Gently wash, pressing with cloth so as not to peel off the aromatic skin.

2

Sprinkle with sake to bring out the aroma.

3

The chicken breast will not stick to the pot if placed on kamaboko.

4

Arrange ingredients colorfully and cover with hot broth.

5

Place the pot on a grill to settle well.

6

As soon as it comes to a boil, add sake.

HOW TO EAT DOBIN-MUSHI

When serving, a sake cup is placed turned down on the lid of the teapot, topped with citrus fruit like sudachi and yuzu. Set aside the citrus fruit and sake cup and uncover the lid of the teapot. Squeeze the citrus fruit a little at a time into the sake cup. Eat the ingredients and the broth alternately.

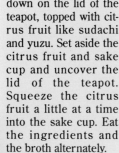

SHUNGIKU WITH WALNUT DRESSING
Shungiku no kurumi-ae

INGREDIENTS

{ 1/2 bunch shungiku
{ (edible leafy chrysanthemum)
{ 1 tsp light soy sauce

3 1/2 oz (100 g) daikon radish
Carrot

Benitade (red smartweed)
Walnut dressing
{ 10 walnut meats
{ 1 Tbsp sake
{ 2 Tbsp sugar
{ 1 Tbsp light soy sauce

Method

① Soak the walnuts in boiling water for 5 minutes. Carefully remove the thin skin with a bamboo skewer.
② Chop with a knife and grind in a mortar until oily. Add the seasonings and mix well.
③ Boil the shungiku quickly in lightly salted water several leaves at a time. Transfer to water to cool. Align in water and then squeeze the water out. Cut into 3/4" (2 cm) lengths. Pour the light soy sauce over and mix lightly.

MOUNTAIN YAM ROLLED IN BEEF
Gyuniku to nagaimo no wain-yaki

INGREDIENTS

8 slices beef (lean meat)
4" (10 cm) mountain yam
16 aojiso (green shiso leaves)
Dash salt & pepper
1 Tbsp vegetable oil

1 1/2 Tbsp soy sauce
1 1/2 Tbsp red wine
1/2 kiku-nori (dried
   chrysanthemum petals)
Prepared mustard

Method
① Wash the mountain yam quickly and pare the thick skin. Cut into 8 sticks, 3/8" (1 cm) square and 4" (10 cm) long.
② Spread the beef on a cutting board lengthwise. Salt and pepper. Place 2 aojiso on it and the yam stick in front. Roll up tightly and secure outside layer with a toothpick.
③ Heat a frying pan and coat with oil. Place the pan on a wet cloth and cool until the sizzling sound dies down. Arrange the beef rolls with the end down.
④ Return the pan to medium heat and fry, shaking the pan, until the whole is browned.
⑤ Sprinkle with soy sauce and wine. Turn up to high and cook until the liquid is almost gone.
⑥ Cut into bite-sized pieces and serve on a plate. Garnish with the kiku-nori, parboiled quickly in vinegared water. Add the prepared mustard at the side.

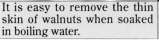

It is easy to remove the thin skin of walnuts when soaked in boiling water.	Use a bamboo skewer to remove the skin in small parts.

④ Cut the daikon and carrot into 2" (5 cm) julienne strips. Place in a bowl and sprinkle with 1/2 tsp salt. Mix lightly all over until watery and then rub with force until soft. Squeeze the excess water out firmly.
⑤ Squeeze the excess water out of the shungiku again. Add the daikon and carrot strips and coat the whole with the walnut dressing. Chill and serve in a bowl topped with benitate.

CHESTNUT RICE
Kuri gohan

INGREDIENTS (4 servings)

2 1/2 cups rice
1/2 cup glutinous rice
20 chestnuts
Toasted black sesame seeds

3 cups kombu stock (see p. 109)
3 Tbsp sake
2/3 tsp salt
2 Tbsp light soy sauce

Grill the chestnuts over a wire net. They become savory, easy to shell and peel.

Method
① Wash the rice (p.102,106) and let stand covered with the kombu stock. Wash the glutinous rice 30 minutes before and soak in 1 cup water.
② Select rather large chestnuts free of worm holes. Cut off the hard bottom.
③ Grill the chestnuts over medium heat, turning occasionally. When darkened and the skin breaks, peel the outer and inner skins together with a cloth.
④ Add drained glutinous rice ①. Add the chestnuts and seasonings and mix. Cook in a rice cooker. When the switch turns off, turn on again and cook until the switch turns off automatically.
⑤ Steam for 10 minutes and then transfer to a flat container. Mix, fluffing up, to remove the excess moisture. Serve in a bowl topped with the black sesame seeds.

Wash the rice more than an hour before cooking and cover with the kombu stock. Prepare the glutinous rice 30 minutes before cooking.

Cut off the hard bottom to prevent bursting open when grilled.

Grill over medium heat, turning, until the skin burns.

Wrap in cloth and peel the outer and inner skins together.

DELICIOUS AND TASTEFUL DISHES

Say "autumn fish" and saury comes to mind. Saury broiled with salt or simmered with ginger and garlic are both delicious. Since it is cooked in vinegared stock for a long time, even the bones become soft. Japanese-style salad is prepared with colorful julienne vegetables dressed with sweet-sour sesame dressing. Voluminous miso soup is full of root vegetables and aburage. It is seasoned with Shinshu-miso and has a plain taste.

SIMMERED SAURY
Sanma no kara-ni

INGREDIENTS

4 sauries	**Simmering stock**
2 cloves garlic	⎧ 3 1/2~4 cups water plus
2 cloves ginger	⎪ kombu soaked water
2 sheets kombu (kelp), 6 × 2"	⎨ 1/2 cup sake
(15 × 5 cm)	⎪ 1/2 cup vinegar
	⎩ 1/3 cup soy sauce

You can store this well-seasoned dish in the refrigerator for 5~6 days, so prepare more than needed to enjoy the taste.

Method

① Scale the sauries and wash quickly in water. Cut off the head from the pectoral fin and the tail. Cut the body into 4 equal portions.

② Push the innards out with a chopstick under running water. Wash in water and pat dry.

③ Wipe the kombu with a dry cloth. Cut into pieces, 3/4" (2 cm) square, with scissors. Soak in 1 cup water for about 30 minutes. Reserve the water for simmering stock.

④ Place the kombu together with the water in a shallow pan. Arrange the fish side by side. Place grated garlic and ginger all over. Cover with water and add the seasonings.

⑤ Bring to a boil over high heat and skim off any scum. Reduce to a medium low heat. Cover with an aluminum foil drop-lid. Simmer for about an hour until the liquid is almost gone.

The innards will be pushed out easily with a chopstick.	The kombu placed on the bottom prevents the fish from scorching.

The quantity of the simmering stock is just enough to cover the fish.	Covered with a drop-lid, boil down until the liquid is almost gone.

JAPANESE-STYLE SALAD
Wafu sarada

INGREDIENTS

7 oz (200 g) daikon radish	**Sesame dressing**
Carrot	⎧ 3 Tbsp neri-goma (sesame
1/2 naganegi	⎪ paste)
Kaiware (daikon sprouts)	⎪ 1 1/2 Tbsp sugar
1 egg for thin omelet	⎨ 1 Tbsp light soy sauce
Suizenji-nori (see p. 115)	⎪ 1 1/2 Tbsp vinegar
	⎩ 2 Tbsp dashi stock

Cut ingredients on hand into beautiful julienne strips and guests will be touched. When the suizenji-nori is unavailable, salted kombu may be substituted.

Method

① Cut the daikon and carrot into 1 1/4" (3 cm) julienne strips. Cut off the roots of kaiware and cut into the same lengths. Cut the naganegi into 1 1/4" (3 cm) lengths. Make a cut lengthwise to remove the core. Cut into julienne strips. Dip all the vegetables into ice water to make crispy.

② Soak the suizenji-nori in water. Cut in the shape of pine leaves.

③ Add a dash of salt to beaten egg. Oil a frying pan lightly and make a thin omelet. Cool in a bamboo colander. Cut in shapes of maple leaves or fans with cutters. If cutters are unavailable, shred the omelet.

④ Drain the vegetables and pile in a bowl. Top with the suizenji-nori and omelet. Combine the ingredients of the sesame dressing in a bowl. Mix well and place at side.

MISO SOUP OF ASSORTED VEGETABLES
Midakusan-jiru

INGREDIENTS

1 3/4 oz (50 g) daikon radish	1/2 aburage
2 taros	(deep-fried tofu)
1 1/4" (3 cm) carrot	2 green onions
1/5 burdock	3 cups dashi stock
1/5 pack shirataki	2 1/8 oz (60 g) miso
(konnyaku noodles)	

Method

① Cut the daikon in a fan shape and the taro in half-moon shape. Wash the burdock with a brush and cut into slices aslant. Soak the daikon and taro in water and the burdock in vinegared water for about 5 minutes to remove harshness.

② Place the shirataki in water and bring it to a boil. Boil for 5 minutes and dip in water. Cut into bite-sized pieces. Pour boiling water over the aburage to remove the excess oil. Cut in half lengthwise and then into thin slices.

③ Add the dashi stock, drained vegetables ① and shirataki to a pan. Cook over high heat. When it comes to a boil, reduce the heat to medium and add the aburage.

④ Cook for 12~13 minutes. Dissolve the miso. When it comes to a boil, scatter chopped green onions and turn off the heat.

To eat with alcoholic beverages
AUTUMN DISHES IN SMALL BOWLS

QUICKLY PICKLED EGGPLANTS
Akinasu no momi-zuke

This is a typical home-made instant pickle flavored with aojiso and myoga. Chill completely before serving.

Ingredients: 2 eggplants / 10 aojiso / 2 myoga (Japanese ginger) / 1 tsp salt

Method
① Cut off the calyx of eggplants and cut into fan-shape slices.
② Cut aojiso leaves in half lengthwise. Roll up and cut into julienne strips from the end. Wash myoga and cut into round thin slices.
③ Put the vegetables in a large bowl and sprinkle with salt. Turning the bowl around, mix and rub lightly. When they get watery, rub with force until tender.
④ Squeeze the water out. Store in the refrigerator until serving.

KIKU-NORI WITH CITRUS FRUIT
Kiku-nori no sudachi-zoe

The sour citrus fruit brings out the taste of slightly sweetened kiku-nori (p.115).

Ingredients: 1 sheet kiku-nori / 2 sudachi (citrus fruit)

Method
① Tear the kiku-nori roughly into pieces and blanch in boiling water with 2~3 drops of vinegared added. Stir once quickly. Transfer to a bamboo colander and fan to cool.
② Squeeze water out. Sprinkle with the juice of citrus fruit and soy sauce.

STIR-FRIED SHIRATAKI AND ENOKI MUSHROOMS
Shirataki to enokidake no iri-ni

Thin ingredients are stir-fried until seasonings are completely absorbed.

Ingredients: 1 pack shirataki (konnyaku noodles) / 1 pack enoki mushrooms / 1 clove ginger / 1 Tbsp sake / 2 Tbsp soy sauce / Dash salt

Method
① Place the shirataki in water in a pan and bring to a boil. After boiling for 5 minutes, dip in water to cool. Drain and cut into bite-sized lengths.
② Cut away root clusters of enoki mushrooms and wash in water. Cut the ginger into julienne strips.
③ Bring the seasonings to a boil in a small pan. Add 2/3 of the ginger, enoki and shirataki. Stir-fry over high heat, stirring continually until the liquid is completely gone.
④ Transfer to a flat container to cool. Serve in a bowl topped with the rest of ginger strips.

MUSHROOMS WITH COD ROE
Kinoko no momijiko-ae

Mushrooms in season have a rich, autumnal flavor. Red cod roe was used to represent red leaves.

Ingredients: 1 pack shimeji mushrooms / 1 pack enoki mushrooms / 3 fresh shiitake mushrooms / 1 lightly salted cod roe / 1 1/3 Tbsp sake / 1 tsp light soy sauce / 4 chives

Method

① Remove the thin skin of cod roe and place in a bowl. Add 1 Tbsp sake and soften.
② Cut away root clusters of the shimeji and enoki and break into pieces. Remove the stems of shiitake and cut into thin slices.
③ Place all the mushrooms in boiling water and bring to a boil. Transfer to a bamboo colander. Fan to cool immediately. Sprinkle with 1/3 Tbsp sake and soy sauce to bring out flavor.
④ Mix the mushrooms with cod roe and serve in a bowl. Top with the chives cut into round thin slices.

SHUNGIKU AND KAMABOKO WITH LEMON SOY SAUCE
Shungiku to kamaboko no remon-joyu

Unusual way of cutting kamaboko makes a fancy dish.

Ingredients: 1 bunch shungiku (edible leafy chrysanthemum) / 1/3 loaf kamaboko (steamed fish-paste cake) / Kimi-soboro (sieved hard-boiled egg yolk) / 2 slices lemon / soy sauce

Method

① Cut off the hard root of the shungiku. Divide into 3~4 groups and parboil individually in lightly salted water .
② Transfer to water to cool. Align in water, take out and squeeze the water out. Cut into 3/4" (2 cm) lengths.
③ Slice the kamaboko horizontally. Pile the slices and cut into fine strips.
④ Mix the shungiku and kamaboko and sprinkle with kimi-soboro. Garnish with lemon slices. Pour lemon juice and soy sauce over before serving.

KIMPIRA OF LOTUS ROOT AND CELERY
Renkon to serori no kimpira

The important point is to cook quickly over high heat so that the food remains firm.

Ingredients: 7 oz (200 g) lotus root / 1 stalk celery / 1 red chili pepper / 1 Tbsp sesame oil / 1/2 Tbsp sake / 1 Tbsp mirin / 1 Tbsp light soy sauce / 1/4 tsp salt

Method

① Pare the thick skin of the lotus root and cut into half-moons(p.10). Soak in vinegared water to remove harshness. Wash in water and drain.
② Remove tough strings from the celery and cut into thin slices. Seed the chili pepper and cut into round thin slices.
③ Heat the oil in a pan and stir-fry the chili pepper and lotus root over high heat.When coated with oil, add the celery and seasonings.
④ Slant the pan and cook until the liquid is completely gone. Transfer to a flat container to cool. Serve in a bowl.

WINTER MENUS

When frost forms, leafy vegetables like spinach and komatsuna (a kind of Chinese cabbage) are in season. Root vegetables like turnip and daikon radish become juicy and increase in sweetness. As for seafood, cod, yellowtail and flounder put on fat.

We long for warm dishes in this season, but vinegared and dressed dishes should be kept cold all the year round.

Winter dishes should be seasoned with less salt than that in summer.

Bring Winter Scenery To The Table

Spinach with Sesame Dressing
Simmered Flounder with Roe
Oysters with Mizore-zu
Tofu and Vegetable Soup
Rice

In winter when the water gets cold, seafood becomes delicious since it puts on fat and the flesh becomes firm. Oysters are dressed with grated and vinegared daikon. Flounder with roe is simmered salty-sweet. Spinach is dressed with sesame of moderate sweetness. The soup of tofu and root vegetables has a rich taste. This is a harmonious winter menu.

SPINACH WITH SESAME DRESSING
Horenso no asaji-ae

INGREDIENTS

1/2 bunch spinach
1 tsp light soy sauce

Sesame dressing
- 2 Tbsp white sesame seeds
- 1/2 Tbsp sake
- 1 Tbsp soy sauce

Toast the sesame seeds, shaking the pan, until crushed easily by finger tips. | Place in a cloth to chop to prevent the seeds from spattering.

Dishes dressed with chopped sesame seeds are called 'asaji-ae.' They are also called 'komachi-ae' in the Kanto region.

Method

① Divide the bunch of spinach in two and parboil half at a time in lightly salted water. Transfer to ice water to cool. Drain and squeeze the water out. Sprinkle with the light soy sauce and set aside

② Toast the sesame seeds over low heat. Place in a dishcloth holding the sides up and chop while hot.

③ Combine the sesame seeds, sake and soy sauce in a bowl. Add the drained spinach cut into 3/4" (2 cm) lengths. Mix well.

SIMMERED FLOUNDER WITH ROE
Komochi-garei no nitsuke

INGREDIENTS

2 fillets flounder with roe
1/3 naganegi (Japanese bunching onion)

Simmering stock
- 1 3/4 cups dashi stock or water
- 3 Tbsp sake
- 3 Tbsp sugar
- 3 Tbsp soy sauce

First, add seasonings to the dashi stock. | Place the fish side by side with serving side up.

When cooking flounder with roe, it is important to use much more simmering stock than usual and simmer for a longer time. Half-done roe will spoil the taste.

Method

① Prepare a flat pan with broad bottom. Bring the dashi stock to a boil over high heat and add the seasonings.

② Add the fish. When the liquid comes to a boil, baste the surface of fish two or three times.

③ Reduce the heat to medium and cover with an aluminum drop-lid. Simmer slowly until liquid reduces 1/3 for about 14~15 minutes.

④ Transfer the fish to a bowl taking care not to break. Cut the naganegi in half lengthwise and then into bite-sized pieces. Cook quickly in the liquid and place in front of the fish. Pour the liquid over the whole.

Baste the fish. | Simmer until liquid reduces 1/3.

MANNERS FOR EATING JAPANESE FOODS

At home you can relax and help yourselves, but on formal occasions you have to mind your manners. It is important to sit up straight. Hold the bowl in your left hand and bring it to your mouth. The posture looks beautiful and it helps to digest food. The following are manners to be kept in mind when eating in the presence of others.

Soups

When the bowl has a lid, hold the bowl with your left hand and take the lid off with your right hand. Turn the lid over and place it at the right side. Sink floating garnishes with chopsticks, take a drink of liquid, enjoying the flavor, and eat ingredients. When finished eating, cover the bowl with the lid.

Sashimi and dressed dishes

When eating sashimi, hold the plate containing soy sauce in your left hand to prevent the soy sauce from dripping. You may either

OYSTERS WITH MIZORE-ZU
Kaki no mizore-zu

1

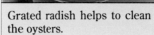

2

Grated radish helps to clean the oysters.

Dip in boiling water until the surface color changes.

INGREDIENTS

12 oysters
1 cup grated daikon radish
1/2 lemon for juice
1/3 bunch seri
　(Japanese parsley)
Carrot
Peel of yuzu citron

Mizore-zu
2 cups grated daikon radish
2 Tbsp vinegar
2 Tbsp sugar
2/3 tsp salt

Method

① Add 1 cup grated daikon to oysters in a bowl. Mix quickly until the daikon turns dark. Remove the dirt and slime completely. Transfer to a bamboo colander and wash under running water, shaking the colander. Drain.
② Bring ample water to a boil in a pan. Dip the oysters together in the colander. Drain while hot and sprinkle with lemon juice. When cooled, chill in the refrigerator.
③ Parboil the seri and cut into 3/4" (2 cm) lengths. Slice the carrot and cut into the shape of a plum blossom with a cutter. Cut the yuzu citron in julienne strips.
④ Make the mizore-zu by combining the ingredients in a bowl. Add the oysters, seri and yuzu citron and mix. Serve in a bowl garnished with carrot.

TOFU AND VEGETABLE SOUP
Kenchin-jiru

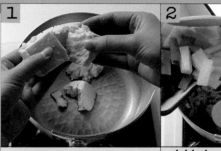

1

2

Crumble the tofu and fry, stirring with a wooden spoon.

Add the vegetables and konnyaku and stir-fry until the whole gets oily.

INGREDIENTS

1/3 block momen-dofu
　(firm tofu)
1 3/4 oz (50g) daikon radish
Carrot
2 taros
1 1/2" (4 cm) burdock
1/4 piece konnyaku
　(devil's tongue jelly)

1/2 naganegi
1 Tbsp vegetable or sesame oil
Broth
3 cups dashi stock
1 tsp salt
1 Tbsp soy sauce

Method

① Wrap the tofu in a dishcloth and make a roll with a bamboo mat. Place a weight on it and let stand for 5~10 minutes to drain.
② Cut the daikon and carrot into 1 1/4" (3 cm) sticks. Cut the taro into the shape of half moon 1/4" (5 mm) thick. Wash completely to remove the slime. Wash the burdock and cut into sasagaki (p.12). Dip in vinegared water for 5 minutes to remove harshness and then wash in water.
③ Place the konnyaku in water and bring it to a boil. After boiling for 5 minutes, transfer to water to make it firm and resilient. Use a spoon to cut into bite-sized pieces.
④ Heat the oil in a pan. Crumble the tofu into the pan and stir-fry quickly over high heat. Add the burdock and fry quickly. Add the daikon, carrot, taro and konnyaku and stir-fry until the whole gets oily.
⑤ Add the dashi stock and bring to a boil and cook over medium heat for 12~13 minutes, skimming the scum as it rises.
⑥ Add the seasonings. Scatter the naganegi cut into round slices 1/4" (5 mm) thick. Turn off the heat.

dissolve wasabi in soy sauce or put it on the sashimi. In the case of dressed dishes, hold the bowl in your left hand and eat.

Simmered dishes
When more than two kinds of food are served together in a bowl, eat heavily seasoned food and lightly ones alternately.

Grilled dishes
When eating a grilled fish, eat the upper flesh bit by bit. When finished, remove the bone in the middle, place it at the further end of the plate and then eat the lower flesh. Never turn the fish over. Bones should be placed neatly together.

Deep-fried dishes
When eating a large tempura like kakiage (mixed tempura, p.54, 55), break up in the bowl into bite-sized pieces with chopsticks.

THE PLEASURES OF COOKING ONE-POT DISHES

Nothing is better than hot dishes when the biting winter wind blows. One-pot dishes full of seafood, meat and vegetables are the best treat to satisfy your stomach. Hot dishes, which we blow on to cool, go well with cold dressed food. Presented here are turnips in season dressed with sweetened vinegar flavored with yuzu citron peel.

SEAFOOD, MEAT AND VEGETABLE POT
Midakusan-nabe

INGREDIENTS

3 fillets fresh cod
6 shrimp
5 1/4 oz (150 g) slices of pork
1/2 block kinugoshi-dofu
  (silken tofu)
1/4 Chinese cabbage
1/3 carrot
2 naganegi
1 bunch seri
  (Japanese parsley)

Broth
⎰5 sheets kombu, 6 × 2"
⎪ (15 × 5 cm)
⎪8 cups water
⎨3 Tbsp sake
⎪1 Tbsp salt
⎱3 Tbsp light soy sauce
Condiments
⎰1/2 bunch chives
⎨1 cup grated daikon radish
⎱Momiji-oroshi (store-bought)

A gorgeous one-pot dish with a variety of ingredients. Enjoy the full rich taste of various ingredients. Cook a little at a time replacing what is eaten.

Method

① Wipe the kombu with a dry cloth and soak in water for about an hour to make kombu stock.
② Cut a cod fillet in half. Devein the shrimp with a bamboo skewer and parboil in lightly salted water until the color turns red.
③ Cut the pork into bite-sized pieces crosswise against the grain. Quarter the tofu.
④ Separate stems and leaves of the Chinese cabbage. Make 2" (5 cm) long julienne stems and coarsely cut leaves. Cut the carrot into fine strips 2" (5 cm) long. Slice the naganegi diagonally. Separate stems and leaves of the seri.
⑤ Heat the kombu dashi in an earthenware pot with a lid. When it comes to a boil, season lightly with the seasonings.
⑥ First, add the cod and pork, and the stems of the Chinese cabbage. Don't add all at once, but bit by bit replacing what is eaten.
⑦ When it comes to a boil, skim off the scum as it rises. Add the naganegi, stems of seri, leaves of cabbage, carrot and tofu and bring to a boil.
⑧ Last, add leaves of seri and shrimp which are easily cooked. Take out food as it is cooked into individual bowls, adding condiments such as sliced chives and momiji-oroshi as desired.

Separate stems and leaves of the Chinese cabbage.

Cook starting with the food which makes good stock and needs time to cook.

Skim the scum carefully as it rises.

After vegetables and tofu are cooked, add leaves of seri and shrimp.

TURNIPS WITH SWEETENED VINEGAR
Kabu no ama-zu

INGREDIENTS

5 small turnips
Yuzu citron peel

Ama-zu (sweetened vinegar)
⎰3 Tbsp vinegar
⎨1 Tbsp sugar
⎱3 Tbsp dashi stock

Method

① Cut off leaves of turnips, leaving about 3/4" (2 cm) of stems intact. Wash with a vegetable brush. Remove dirt between stems carefully under running water.
② Without peeling, cut in half lengthwise and then into thin slices.
③ Place in a bowl and sprinkle with 1/2 tsp salt. Rub until soft and watery. Squeeze the water out tightly.
④ Combine the ingredients of ama-zu. Add the turnips and mix well. Store chilled in the refrigerator until serving.
⑤ Serve in a bowl. Scatter the julienne strips of yuzu citron peel over.

WINTER DISHES IN SMALL BOWLS

FRUITS DRESSED WITH GRATED DAIKON
Furutsu no yukimi-ae

A refreshing combination of fruits and grated daikon radish, which should be juicy.

Ingredients: 1 kiwi fruit / 1/4 papaya / 1 cup grated daikon with juice / 1 Tbsp sugar / 1 Tbsp vinegar / 1/4 tsp salt / 1 1/2 Tbsp white wine

Method
① Pare the kiwi fruit and cut into 3/8" (1 cm) cubes. Pare and seed the papaya and cut into fan-shape slices.
② Place the grated daikon in a bowl and add the seasonings, wine and fruits. Mix quickly together.
③ Chill the mixture until serving colorfully in a bowl.

VINEGARED DRIED DAIKON STRIPS
Kiriboshi-daikon no sunomono

If you find crisp white kiriboshi (dried daikon strips) in the market, try this vinegared dish.

Ingredients: 1 oz (30 g) kiriboshi-daikon (dried daikon strips) / Komatsuna (a kind of Chinese cabbage) / **Awase-zu** <1/2 cup vinegar / 2 Tbsp sugar / 1 Tbsp light soy sauce / Dash salt / 1/2 cup dashi stock>

Method
① Wash the daikon strips quickly in water and soak in ample water for 15 minutes. Drain and squeeze the excess water out.
② Combine the seasonings of awase-zu in a bowl. Dress the daikon strips with the mixture. Store chilled in the refrigerator for half a day to season.
③ Garnish with the komatsuna parboiled in salted water.

TARO AND LOTUS ROOT WITH NANBAN-ZU
Satoimo to renkon no nanban-zu

A tasteful dish of deep-fried taro and lotus root. They should be soaked in nanban-zu immediately while hot.

Ingredients: 3 taros / 3 1/2 oz (100 g) lotus root / Dash cornstarch / **Nanban-zu** <1 red chili pepper / 1/2 cup vinegar / 1/2 tsp salt / 1 1/2 Tbsp light soy sauce / 1/2 cup dashi stock> / Chives / Oil for deep-frying

Method
① Pare the thick skin of the lotus root and taro. Cut both into round slices 1/4" (5 mm) thick. Dip the lotus root in vinegared water to remove harshness. Wash in water quickly. Drain.
② Make the nanban-zu by combining the chili pepper seeded and cut into round thin slices, the seasonings and dashi stock.
③ Sprinkle a dash of salt over the vegetables and coat lightly with cornstarch. Deep-fry in 330°F (165°C) oil.
④ When the taro is done, soak the whole in the nanban-zu and let stand for 30 minutes, stirring occasionally. Serve in a bowl garnished with the chives.

TOSA-NI OF BURDOCK
Gobo no tosa-ni

Burdock is rich in dietary fibers and good for health. Tosa-ni is a name given to the dish which uses bonito flakes.

Ingredients: 5 1/4 oz (150 g) burdock / **Simmering stock** < 3/4 cup dashi stock / 2 Tbsp mirin / 1 1/2 Tbsp soy sauce> / 3/8 oz (10 g) bonito flakes

Method
① Wash the burdock with a vegetable brush. Cut diagonally into slices 1/8" (3 mm) thick. Soak in vinegared water to remove harshness until the water turns brown. Wash in water and drain.
② Toast the bonito flakes over low heat until completely dried. Transfer to a flat container and crush with hands.
③ Place the burdock and simmering stock in a pan and cook over high heat. When it comes to a boil, reduce the heat to medium and simmer, stirring until the liquid is gone.
④ Transfer to a flat container. Sprinkle the bonito flakes over while hot and mix well quickly.

ISOBE-AE OF BOILED SPINACH
Horenso no isobe-ae

Spinach is best to eat around the first frost. Isobe is a name given to a dish which uses nori seaweed.

Ingredients: 1/2 bunch spinach / **Dashi mixture** < 3/4 cup dashi stock / 1 Tbsp light soy sauce> / 1/2 sheet toasted nori / Kimi-soboro (sieved hard-boiled egg yolk)

Method
① Wash the spinach thoroughly back and forth in cold water. Divide into 2~3 groups and parboil each in salted water, retaining firmness. Dip in ice water.
② Squeeze the excess water out tightly. Soak in the dashi mixture in a flat container. Chill in the refrigerator for 30 minutes to season.
③ Squeeze the liquid lightly. Cut into 3/4" (2 cm) lengths and quarter the hard end.
④ Crush the nori sheet with hands and sprinkle over the spinach. Serve in a bowl topped with the kimi-soboro.

INSTANT PICKLE OF CHINESE CABBAGE
Hakusai no sokuseki-zuke

The Chinese cabbage is rubbed with salt and coated with vinegar mixture. This can be preserved for a long time.

Ingredients: 3 leaves (10 1/2 oz /300 g) Chinese cabbage / 1 tsp salt / **Vinegar mixture** < 1/2 cup vinegar / 1 1/2 Tbsp sugar / Dash salt / 1/2 Tbsp light soy sauce / 1 Tbsp sesame oil / 1 red chili pepper>

Method
① Separate the leaves and stems of the Chinese cabbage. Cut the stems into bars lengthwise and leaves into bite-sized pieces.
② Place the cabbage in a bowl and sprinkle with salt. Rub lightly until tender.
③ Seed the chili pepper and cut into round thin slices. Make the vinegar mixture by combining the chili pepper and the seasonings. Bring it to a boil.
④ Pour the hot vinegar mixture over the Chinese cabbage. Mix well and chill.

EACH CONTAINER has its OWN FRONT VIEW

● The side near you in the photos is the front.

Square plate

The side near you is the front. A rectangular plate is placed sideways.

Half-moon plate

The straight side is the front.

Hexagonal plate

The corner is the front.

Lipped bowl

Direct the lip to the left.

Octagonal plate

The side is the front.

Dented bowl

Direct the dent to the left.

Rhombic plate

The corner is the front. It is placed sideways.

Gourd-shaped bowl

Direct the pointed part to the left.

In principle, containers should be placed the way they look stable and pleasant to the eye. If the container has a picture, the correct side of the picture comes to the front.

When serving food, the container should be placed with the front directed to the guest. The front of some containers is set, so they should be placed as designated.

Bowl shaped like the fruit of Japanese pepper

Direct the notch toward you.

Leaf-shaped plate

Direct the tip of the leaf to the left sideways.

Petal-shaped bowl

The joint of petals is the front.

Raised corner plate

A corner of the plate is raised. Place so that the raised corner comes to the upper right with the designs facing front.

Wooden bowl

In principle, the side with brilliant pictures is the front. A bowl with a pattern or two has the pattern in the front. Where there are three patterns, the space between the patterns is the front.

Tray

Trays of Japanese cedar or lacquered ware are placed with the grain sideways. When the side has a joint, a round tray should be placed with the joint in front and the joint of a square tray comes at the back.

Add flavor and decorative color to the food.

GARNISHES

Sudori-shoga

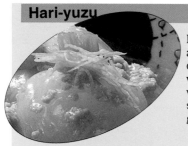

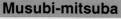

Sudori-shoga is a young ginger shoot soaked in sweet vinegar. It is used as a garnish for grilled dishes. Make one from the three shapes – pestle, brush and fan. Dip in boiling water, coat with salt and let stand for 5 minutes. Wash in water and soak in equal amounts of vinegar and water for 5 minutes.

Pestle

Brush

Fan

Kinome

Kinome is the fragrant young leaves of a prickly ash tree. Cup your hands, place the leaves in the palm and join the hands repeatedly as if clapping to bring out the flavor. They are good in soups and placed on top of dressed dishes.

Hari-yuzu

Hari-yuzu are strips of yuzu citrus peel. They are placed on top of simmered and dressed dishes or put in soups to give refreshing flavor. Pare the skin about 3/4" (2 cm) wide sideways. Scrape off the bitter fuzz on the backside. Cut off the four sides to make a rectangle and cut it in julienne strips from the end.

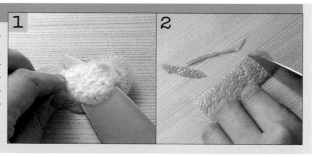

Musubi-mitsuba

Musubi-mitsuba are tied honeworts often called 'Japanese parsley.' They are used in soups and for garnishes for chawan-mushi (steamed egg custard). The word 'tie' suggests 'forming a connection,' so they are used on celebratory occasions. Pound the white parts of the stems lightly and make a ring. Insert the leaves through it and tie.

Momiji-oroshi

Momiji-oroshi is grated daikon radish with a red chili pepper. It is used for one-pot dishes and steamed fish as a pungent condiment. Cut the daikon in a thick round slice and make a hole in the middle with a chopstick. Insert a seeded red chili pepper into it. Store in the refrigerator for half a day to make the pepper soft and then grate them together.

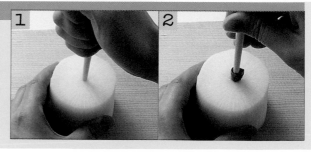

DECORATIVE CUTS

Decorative cut garnishes give a sense of the seasons to dishes. Their appearance in containers creates a pleasant atmosphere and makes the dishes tastier.
It is delightful to decorate the dishes using with your own ideas.

Peels of Yuzu Citron

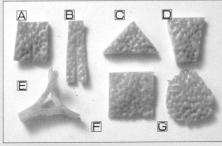

(A) (B) Pine needles
(C) Scale (D) Wedge
(E) Twisted pine needles
(F) Paper (G) Flake

Twisted pine needles

(A) (B) Make a lengthwise cut in square or rectangular peel.

(E) Make cuts alternately in a rectangular peel. Open and twist and make a triangle as shown in the photo.

Form shapes, triangle (C), square (F) and trapezoid (D).

(G) Shave off the peel.

There are no fixed rules for the use of these cuts.

Snake's Eye (Janome)

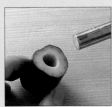

Use cylinder-like vegetables like cucumber and pickling melon. Remove the center using an apple core or cutter and discard. Cut the vegetable into round slices from the end. The thickness depends on the dish.

Cut-out Patterns

Using cutters, cut vegetables into the shapes of a cherry blossom in spring, leaves of ginkgo and maple in autumn and ume in winter. Cut carrot or daikon radish into 1/8" (3 mm) thick slices. Place cloth on the cutter and press to cut out the patterns. Parboil quickly in boiling water. Also cut out a thin omelet or vinegared ginger in the same way for garnishes.

Twisted Ume Blossom

Make a red blossom with carrot and a white blossom with daikon radish. Cut the vegetable into 1/4" (5 mm) thick slices. Cut out with a cutter of ume blossom. Score divisions between each of the five petals. Cut away a small wedge along each petal to give a three-dimensional effect. Parboil quickly.

Cucumber Stand

Garnish sashimi with wasabi horseradish on this stand. It creates an attractive display. Slice one end to make a flat bottom and then make three cuts diagonally. Twist and pull apart. It is also used as a stand for grated ginger and garlic.

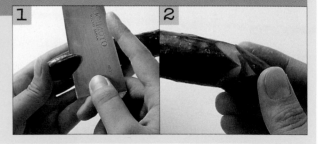

PREPARATION of SEAFOOD

TWO-PIECE CUT and THREE-PIECE CUT

Fish with entrails are perishable, so remove them immediately when bought, wash the whole in water and store in the refrigerator on a flat container. When filleting, steady the fish with finger tips of the left hand.

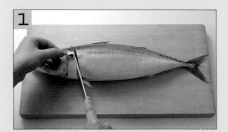

Lay the fish, turning the head to your left. Insert a knife under the pectoral fin and cut towards the head until you reach the backbone. Turn over, repeat and cut off the head.

Remove the head, pulling the entrails out at the same time with both hands.

Insert a finger into the belly and wash away under running water remaining entrails and blood. Rinse the whole briefly and wipe dry the outside and inside with a tightly wrung dishcloth.

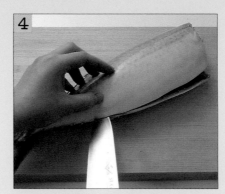

Lay the fish, turning the head part to your right and belly side towards you. Split the belly down to the vent.

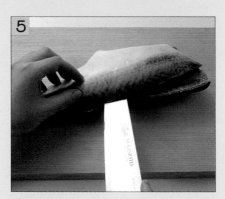

Turn over. Cut open just above the bones down to the tail, keeping the blade of the knife flat.

Cut into two pieces, one with bones and the other without bones. This is called 'nimai-oroshi.'

To make a three-piece cut, lay the fillet with the backbone, bone side down. Insert a knife just above the bone and slide it along the backbone.

You now have three fillets, two without bones and one with the backbone. This is called 'sanmai-oroshi.' The backbone is used for soup.

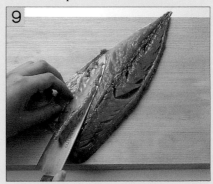

Cut off the remaining bones on the belly side, inserting the knife diagonally. When making vinegared mackerel, carefully pick out bones.

SQUID

Squid and cuttlefish are most popular among the members of the cephalopod mollusk.

Cuttlefish is usually available opened, so presented here is the preparation of squid.

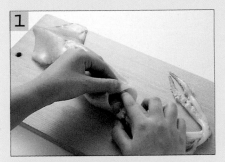

The tentacles are connected at the end of the body. Lift the body a little, insert fingers and separate.

Hold the body and tentacles with each hand and pull out. The innards come out together with the tentacles.

Remove the cartilage. Wash quickly in water and clean the inside of the body.

Insert the thumb between the head and body and tear starting from the body.

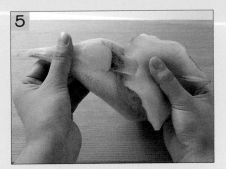

Pull the head down. Part of the skin comes out together with the head.

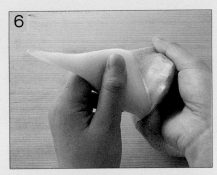

Peel the rest of the skin starting at the end of the body. Pull down it all at once.

Cut open the body with a knife.

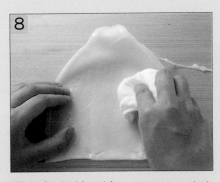

Wipe the inside with a wrung-out cloth and remove the slime.

TENTACLES

Tentacles can be broiled with salt or deep-fried. After the sac of black ink is removed, sprinkle salt over the innards and broil wrapped in aluminum foil. Cut into fine strips and mix with the strips of body. It makes an instant shiokara (salted fish guts).

① Separate the tentacles and innards.
② Cut between eyes.
③ Remove the eyes and beak in water.
④ Cut the tentacles in the same length. Separate into two each. Remove suckers.

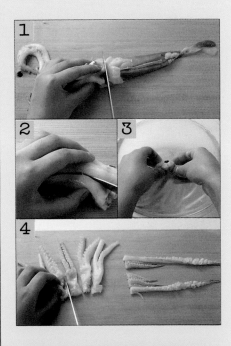

HEAD

It is firm and tasty. You can use it for sashimi or parboil and cut into fine strips for dressed dishes and salads.

① Make a shallow score at the top.
② Pick the end and peel the skins of both sides.

SHRIMP

HOW TO DEVEIN

Shrimp has a black intestinal vein at the back. Sand is sometimes contained in it and it is unpleasant to the tongue. You have to remove it before cooking. There are two methods of removing the vein as follows.

1
When retaining the head, curve the body and insert a bamboo skewer between second and third joints from the head. Pull out the vein with the support of the forefinger. Shelled shrimp is also deveined in the same way.

2
When a headless shrimp is used, place it on its back on a board. Make a cut at the head joint as far as the shell below. Pull the head and body to right and left with hands. The vein is removed together with the head.

HOW TO SHELL

Remove shells by peeling from the belly side along the body. Leave the shell to one joint away from the tail. It turns bright red when cooked and is pleasant to the eye.

BEFORE DEEP-FRYING

Watery shrimp splashes oil when deep-frying and is very dangerous. Remove the moisture of the surface and cut off the hard parts of the tail tip since they are watery. The water contained in the tail should be removed with a knife. If you make a few cuts on the belly side crosswise, the shrimp will not warp when fried.

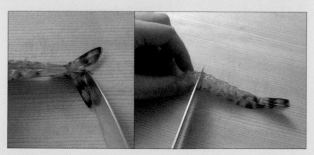

SHELLFISH

SHELLED SHELLFISH

Place in a bamboo colander and put in a bowl of water. Pick up remaining shells with fingers. Wash completely under running water, shaking the colander, to remove the slime and dirt.

LITTLENECK CLAM, CORBICULAE

Littleneck clam (asari) live in the shoals. Their season is from winter to early spring. Corbiculae (shijimi) lives in fresh water like rivers and lakes. They are available both in summer and winter. Dip the asari in salted water and shijimi in fresh water to excrete any sand they contain. Wash the shells, rubbing under running water, before cooking.

CLAMS

Clams have valves. Their season is from March to April. The sand of store-bought clams are already excreted. To test for freshness, hit two clams together. If they make a clean, hard sound, they are fresh. Those which make a dull sound are dead. Discard them. Wash and scrub with a cooking brush under running water and remove dirt before cooking.

BASIC STOCK and DRESSINGS (2 servings)

SIMMERING STOCK FOR FISH

For ordinary simmering, salty-sweet, thick stock is used. For quick cooking, thin and ample stock is used. Blue fishes like mackerel, sardine and horse mackerel, have strong smells and they are not suitable for quick cooking. If you add ginger, pickled ume or Japanese pepper seeds to the simmering stock, you can get rid of the odor and appreciate and enjoy the taste of those fishes.

STOCK FOR WHITE FISH
1/2 cup dashi stock / 1 Tbsp sake / 1 1/2 Tbsp sugar / 1 1/2 Tbsp mirin / 2 Tbsp soy sauce

QUICK COOKING OF WHITE FISH
1 cup dashi stock / 2 Tbsp sake / 1/2 Tbsp sugar / 1/2 Tbsp mirin / 4 Tbsp soy sauce

STOCK FOR BLUE FISH
3/4 cup dashi stock / 1 1/2 Tbsp sake / 1 1/2 Tbsp sugar / 1 1/2 Tbsp mirin / 2 1/2 Tbsp soy sauce

SIMMERING STOCK FOR VEGETABLES

LIGHTLY SEASONED
1 cup dashi stock / 1 Tbsp sake / 1/2 Tbsp sugar / 1/2 Tbsp mirin / 1 Tbsp light soy sauce

SALTY-SWEET
3/4 cup dashi stock / 1 Tbsp sake / 2 Tbsp sugar / 1 Tbsp mirin / 2 Tbsp soy sauce

NIBITASHI (for long simmering)
1 cup dashi stock / 1 Tbsp sake / 2 Tbsp mirin / 1 Tbsp light soy sauce / Dash salt

TERIYAKI SAUCE

Sweet sauce is suitable for yellow tail and Spanish mackerel which have rich fat. Salty sauce is good for cutlass fish and tuna which have a plain taste.

Sweet
4 Tbsp soy sauce / 3 Tbsp sake / 3 Tbsp mirin

Salty
5 Tbsp soy sauce / 3 Tbsp sake / 2 Tbsp mirin

AWASE-ZU (Vinegar mixture)

Adjust the taste in accordance with the main dishes and seasons. In spring and summer, a plain taste is desirable and in autumn and winter, a sweetish taste. If you add shoga (ginger), karashi (prepared mustard) and grated wasabi horseradish to nihai-zu, you can obtain shoga-zu, karashi-zu and wasabi-zu respectively. Adding goma (sesame seeds) to sanbai-zu yields goma-zu. Kinome (young leaves of prickly ash) may be added to either nihai-zu or sanbai-zu as desired.

NIHAI-ZU
Sweet
1 1/2 Tbsp vinegar / 1 Tbsp sugar / 1 Tbsp light soy sauce / 1 Tbsp dashi stock
Plain
1 1/2 Tbsp vinegar / 1 1/2 Tbsp light soy sauce / 2 Tbsp dashi stock

SANBAI-ZU
Sweet
1 1/2 Tbsp vinegar / 2/3 Tbsp sugar / 1/2 Tbsp light soy sauce / 1 1/2 Tbsp dashi stock / Dash salt
Plain
1 1/2 Tbsp vinegar / 1 tsp sugar / 1/2 Tbsp light soy sauce / 1 1/2 Tbsp dashi stock / Dash salt

PON-ZU SHOYU
3 Tbsp citrus fruit juice / 2~3 Tbsp soy sauce

INDEX

Aburage
Nibitashi of Komatsuna and Aburage
......................................30
Stuffed Tofu Puff Sushi....................100
Miso Soup of Assorted Vegetables
......................................139

Age-boru
Oden..............................92

Aojiso
Deep-fried Chicken with Aojiso.......128
String Beans Wrapped in Shiso
......................................133

Ark shell
Ark Shells and Rape Blossoms with
Nihai-zu 67

Asparagus
Soy-steeped Asparagus and Shiitake
......................................77
Miso Soup of Asparagus and Udo ...110

Bakudaikai
(Unique Ingredients) 115

Bamboo shoot
Bamboo Shoot and Cuttlefish
with Kinome-miso 71
Tosa-ni of Bamboo Shoot and
Butterbur 120
Clear Bamboo Shoot Soup 121

Beef
Braised Beef and Potatoes 16
Beef Tataki....................................44
Sukiyaki...90
Beef, Broad Beans and Udo.............123
Mountain Yam Rolled in Beef.........137

Bluefish
Chiri-mushi of Bluefish 63

Bonito flakes
Wheat Noodles with Bonito Flakes 104
(Dashi Stock) 108
Bonito Flakes in Green Peppers......132

Bracken
Pounded Bracken............................124

Broad beans
Udo and Broad Beans in Ume Dressing 69
Vegetable Soup................................112
Beef, Broad Beans and Udo.............123

Buckweat noodles
Buckwheat Noodles with Tempura 104

Burdock
Burdock Kimpira..............................29
Tempura...51
Miso Soup of Gurnard and Burdock
......................................111

Vegetable Soup.................................112
Miso Soup of Assorted Vegetables 139
Tosa-ni of Burdock........................149

Butterbur
Octopus and Butterbur with
Karashi-zu 69
Vegetable Soup................................112
Tosa-ni of Bamboo Shoot and
Butterbur 120

Cabbage
Cabbage and Radishes Squeezed
with Salt............................122
Cabbage Simmered with Vinegar....124

Carrot
Tempura...51
Mixed Sushi....................................96
Vegetable Soup................................112
Japanese-style Salad.........................139

Celery
Dressed Summer Vegetable Cubes
......................................132
Kimpira of Lotus Root and Celery ...141

Chestnut
Chestnut Rice 137

Chicken
Braised Chicken...............................14
Simmered Turnips with Minced
Chicken 26
Chicken Teriyaki..............................45
Steamed Egg Custard 60
Assorted Casserole 88
Mitsuba and Chicken with Wasabi
Vinegar 125
Deep-fried Chicken with Aojiso.......128

Chikuwa
Variations of Mixed Tempura...........55
Oden..92

Chinese cabbage
Nibitashi of Chinese Cabbage and
Littleneck Clams 31
Instant Pickle of Chinese Cabbage 149

Clam
Assorted Casserole 88
Pan-fried Clams...............................123
(Preparation of Seafood) 156

Cod
Seafood, Meat and Vegetable Pot....147

Cod roe
Mushrooms with Cod Roe 141

Corbicula
(Preparation of Seafood) 156
Miso Soup of Corbiculae 128

Cowpeas
Red Bean Rice 101

Cucumber
Cucumber and Wakame with
Sanbai-zu 67
Cuttlefish and Cucumber with
Kimi-zu 68
Dressed Greens................................128
Dressed Summer Vegetable Cubes
......................................132

Cuttlefish
Broiled Cuttlefish with Egg Yolk.......41
Tempura...51
Variations of Mixed Tempura...........55
Cuttlefish and Cucumber with
Kimi-zu 68
Bamboo Shoot and Cuttlefish with
Kinome-miso 71
Sashimi...80

Daikon radish
Simmered Pork with Daikon Radish
......................................24
Dried Strips of Daikon Radish...........34
Oden..92
Japanese-style Salad.........................139
Miso Soup of Assorted Vegetables 139

Daikon strips
Vinegared Dried Daikon Strips 148

Egg
Kamaboko and Mitsuba Cooked
with Eggs 27
Thick Omelets..................................46
Omelets with Fillings.........................47
Steamed Egg Custard 60
Oden..92
Mixed Sushi....................................96
Mushrooms and Curdled Egg Soup
......................................113
Japanese-style Salad.........................139

Eggplant
Nabe-shigi of Eggplant 28
Tempura...51
Grilled Eggplants.............................131
Dressed Summer Vegetable Cubes
......................................132
Quickly Pickled Eggplants..............140

Enoki mushroom
Stir-fried Shirataki and Enoki
Mushrooms 140
Mushrooms with Cod Roe 141

Fine noodles
Fine Noodles 104

Fish
(Preparation of Seafood) 154
Flatfish
Flatfish Cooked Quickly.....................20
Flounder
Simmered Flounder with Roe..........144
Ganmodoki
Oden 92
Ginkgo Nuts
(Unique Ingredients) 115
Green onion
Miso Soup of Assorted Vegetables 139
Green peas
Green Peas Thickened with Kuzu...124
Green pepper
Bonito Flakes in Green Peppers......132
Gurnard
Miso Soup of Gurnard and Burdock 111
Harusame
(Reconstitution of Dry Goods) 35
Sea Bass and Harusame Soup 112
Hijiki
Hijiki Mixed with Vegetables 33
Honewort
Mitsuba and Chicken with Wasabi
    Vinegar.......................................125
Horse mackerel
Salt-broiled Horse Mackerel.............38
Horse Mackerel and Negi
    with Su-miso 72
Chopped Horse Mackerel.................85
Iriko
(Dashi Stock) 109
Kaiware
Japanese-style Salad...........................139
Kamaboko
Kamaboko and Mitsuba Cooked
    with Eggs 27
Shungiku and Kamaboko with
    Lemon Soy Sauce 141
Kampyo
(Reconstitution of Dry Goods) 35
Mixed Sushi.......................................96
Thick Sushi Rolls 98
Kidney beans
Simmered Kidney Beans....................32
Kiku-nori
(Unique Ingredients) 115
Kiku-nori with Citrus Fruit..............140
Kinmedai
Simmered Kinmedai 22
Assorted Casserole 88

Kinome
(Garnishes) 152
Variations of Broiled Foods 43
Kiwi fruit
Fruits Dressed with Grated Daikon 148
Kobashira
Mixed Tempura of Kobashira and
    Mitsuba 54
Komatsuna
Nibitashi of Komatsuna and
    Aburage..30
Kombu
Oden 92
Mixed Sushi.......................................96
(Dashi Stock) 108
Konnyaku
Oden 92
Lettuce
Nibitashi of Lettuce and Young
    Sardines..31
Littleneck clam
Nibitashi of Chinese Cabbage and
    Littleneck Clams 31
(Preparation of Seafood) 156
Lotus root
Tempura...51
Mixed Sushi.......................................96
Kimpira of Lotus Root and Celery ...141
Taro and Lotus Root with Nanban-zu
   148
Mackerel
Simmered Mackerel in Miso 23
Vinegared Mackerel 84
Matsutake mushroom
Matsutake Mushrooms in a Teapot
   136
Mitsuba
Kamaboko and Mitsuba Cooked
    with Eggs 27
Mixed Tempura of Kobashira
    and Mitsuba 54
Variations of Mixed Tempura...........55
Soy-steeped Mitsuba..........................77
Mitsuba and Chicken with Wasabi
    Vinegar.......................................125
Mountain yam
Mountain Yam with Ume Flesh.......133
Mountain Yam Rolled in Beef.........137
Myoga
Dressed Greens.................................128
Miso Soup of String Beans and
    Myoga 131

Naganegi
Variations of Mixed Tempura...........55
Horse Mackerel and Negi with
    Su-miso...72
Japanese-style Salad...........................139
Nori seaweed
Tempura...50
Thick Sushi Rolls 98
Okra
Miso Soup of Okra and Tofu............110
Onion
Variations of Mixed Tempura...........55
Octopus
Octopus and Butterbur with Karashi-zu 69
Oyster
Oysters with Mizore-zu 145
Papaya
Fruits Dressed with Grated Daikon
   148
Pickling melon
Vinegared Pickling Melon 132
Pomfret
Broiled Pomfret in Saikyo-way 42
Pond smelt
Deep-fried Pond Smelts in Nanban-zu
   57
Pork
Simmered Pork with Daikon Radish
   24
Deep-fried Marinated Pork 55
Seafood, Meat and Vegetable Pot....147
Potato
Braised Beef and Potatoes 16
Oden 92
Radish
Cabbage and Radishes Squeezed
    with Salt.....................................122
Rape blossom
Ark Shells and Rape Blossoms
    with Nihai-zu.................................67
Rape Blossoms Dressed in
    Soy Sauce with Mustard 75
Rape Blossoms and Udo in
    Karashi-zu 120
Rice
Red Bean Rice 101
Rice with Vegetables.......................102
Ume Rice...128
Chestnut Rice 137
Round clam
Round Clams and Scallions with
    Karashi Su-miso...........................70

Sardine
Nibitashi of Lettuce and Young
    Sardines.................................31
Satsuma-age
Oden 92
Saury
Simmered Saury....................139
Scabbard fish
Grilled Scabbard Fish 121
Scallion
Round Clams and Scallions with
    Karashi Su-miso...................70
Scallop
Scallops and Vegetable Soup 113
Sea bass
Sea Bass and Harusame Soup 112
Sea Bass 131
Sea bream
Sashimi.....................................80
Shellfish
(Preparation of Seafood) 156
Shiitake mushroom
(Reconstitution of Dry Goods) 35
Soy-steeped Asparagus and Shiitake
   77
Mixed Sushi...............................96
Thick Sushi Rolls 98
(Dashi Stock) 109
Vegetable Soup..........................112
Mushrooms with Cod Roe 141
Shimeji mushroom
Miso Soup of Shimeji Mushrooms
    and Tofu.............................111
Mushrooms and Curdled Egg Soup
   113
Mushrooms with Cod Roe 141
Shirataki
Miso Soup of Assorted Vegetables 139
Stir-fried Shirataki and Enoki
    Mushrooms...................................140
Shrimp
Assortment of Simmered Foods........18
Tempura....................................51
Variations of Mixed Tempura...........55
Mixed Sushi...............................96
Wax Gourd and Shrimp..................129
Seafood, Meat and Vegetable Pot....147
(Preparation of Seafood) 156
Shungiku
Shungiku with Walnut Dressing 136
Shungiku and Kamaboko with
    Lemon Soy Sauce 141

Sillago
Tempura....................................51
Snow peas
Mixed Sushi......................................96
Soybeans
Dressed Greens..............................128
Spanish mackerel
Spanish Mackerel with Yuan-jiru 40
Spinach
Spinach with Sesame Dressing 74
Soy-steeped Spinach 76
Spinach with Sesame Dressing 144
Isobe-ae of Boiled Spinach 149
Squash
Sweetened Squash 131
Squid
Sashimi.....................................80
(Preparation of Seafood) 155
String beans
String Beans with Sesame Dressing
   75
Miso Soup of String Beans and
    Myoga.............................131
String Beans Wrapped in Shiso.......133
Sudachi
Kiku-nori with Citrus Fruit..............140
Sudori-shoga
(Garnishes) 152
Suizenji-nori
(Unique Ingredients) 115
Sweet pepper
Tempura....................................51
Dressed Greens..............................128
Sweet potato
Tempura....................................51
Taranome
Taranome with Sesame Dressing....125
Taro
Miso Soup of Assorted Vegetables 139
Taro and Lotus Root with Nanban-zu
   148
Tilefish
Steamed Tilefish and Turnip.............62
Tofu
(Reconstitution of Dry Goods) 35
Deep-fried Puffy Tofu 56
Tofu Dressing...................................72
Miso Soup of Okra and Tofu...........110
Miso Soup of Shimeji Mushrooms
    and Tofu.............................111
Chilled Tofu 133
Tofu and Vegetable Soup 145

Tomato
Dressed Summer Vegetable Cubes
   132
Tuna
Sashimi.....................................80
Turnip
Simmered Turnips with Minced Chicken
   26
Steamed Tilefish and Turnip.............62
Chrysanthemum Turnip in Ama-zu
   66
Turnips with Sweetened Vinegar 147
Udo
Udo and Broad Beans in Ume Dressing
   69
Miso Soup of Asparagus and Udo ...110
Vegetable Soup..........................112
Rape Blossoms and Udo in
    Karashi-zu.........................120
Beef, Broad Beans and Udo............123
Kimpira of Udo Skin 125
Ume
Ume Rice....................................128
Mountain Yam with Ume Flesh.......133
Wakame
(Reconstitution of Dry Goods)
   35
Cucumber and Wakame with Sanbai-zu
   67
Walnut
Shungiku with Walnut Dressing 136
Wax gourd
Wax Gourd and Shrimp..................129
Wheat noodles
Wheat Noodles with Bonito Flakes
   104
Yaki-dofu
Oden 92
Yellowtail
Salt-broiled Yellowtail 39
Yuri-ne
(Unique Ingredients) 115
Zenmai
(Reconstitution of Dry Goods) 35
Simmered Zenmai.............................122